THE PERSONALIZED
HIGH SCHOOL

THE PERSONALIZED HIGH SCHOOL

Making Learning Count for Adolescents

Joseph A. DiMartino
Denise L. Wolk
EDITORS

Contributing Authors: Paul Curtis,
Catherine DeLaura, Ricardo Leblanc-Esparza,
Virginia Eves, Linda Nathan, Ron Newell,
Debbie Osofsky, Jeff Park, Teri Schrader,
and Mark Van Ryzin

Foreword by George H. Wood

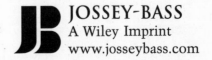

JOSSEY-BASS
A Wiley Imprint
www.josseybass.com

Published by Jossey-Bass

A Wiley Imprint

989 Market Street, San Francisco, CA 94103-1741—www.josseybass.com

Jossey-Bass books and products are available through most bookstores. To contact Jossey-Bass directly call our Customer Care Department within the U.S. at 800-956-7739, outside the U.S. at 317-572-3986, or fax 317-572-4002.

Jossey-Bass also publishes its books in a variety of electronic formats. Some content that appears in print may not be available in electronic books.

Library of Congress Cataloging-in-Publication Data
The personalized high school : making learning count for adolescents / edited by Joseph A. DiMartino, Denise L. Wolk ; contributing authors, Paul Curtis . . . [et al.] ; foreword by George Wood. — 1st ed.
   p. cm.
Includes bibliographical references and index.
ISBN 978-0-7879-9489-1 (pbk.)
  1. High school teaching—United States—Case studies. 2. Individualized instruction—United States—Case studies. 3. School improvement programs—United States—Case studies. I. DiMartino, Joseph. II. Wolk, Denise, 1959- III. Curtis, Paul, teacher.
LB1607.5.P47 2010
373.139'4—dc22

2010003899

Printed in the United States of America

FIRST EDITION

PB Printing   10 9 8 7 6 5 4 3 2 1

CONTENTS

For Mick DiMartino

We have often said that we learned much more from our children than they could ever hope to learn from us. Mick provided us with a lesson in dying with grace and dignity that will be with us for all our days. He is sorely missed.

For Ted Sizer

Whose life and work championing progressive educational ideals will continue to affect hundreds of thousands of educators and students. He was a mentor and friend to us all.

ACKNOWLEDGMENTS

Over the past several years, we've had the chance to meet hundreds of dedicated teachers, principals, administrators, and community leaders who have worked hard to create educational experiences that embrace the challenge of educating students in the new millennium. When we set out to put this book together, we asked people we knew in some of these unique schools to contribute their stories.

We first approached Jossey-Bass with the idea for *The Personalized High School: Making Learning Count for Adolescents* as a sequel to our book *Personalized Learning: Preparing High School Students to Create Their Futures,* which we worked on with our colleague and friend John Clarke. Schools from across the country are highlighted throughout this book to exemplify various strategies of high school reform. Just as the *Personalized Learning* book was a collection of writings by practitioners, so is *The Personalized High School* a collection of experiences written by practitioners for their colleagues in other schools who are embarking or continuing on their road to improving teaching and learning at their schools. And since students are at the core of all personalization efforts, we have invited students to provide their own perspectives on change wherever we could.

With that in mind, we would like to thank all of the practitioner-authors who have contributed to this book, as well as the student contributors, because without all of you we simply would not have a story. We would also like to thank our editorial and production team from Jossey-Bass: Christie Hakim, Kate Gagnon, Julia Parmer, and Justin Frahm for their patience and guidance in getting our book out of the trenches and into print. We thank our spouses for their unwavering support, and all of our children for demonstrating to us every day what teaching and learning really is—a continuing journey of change.

FOREWORD

Every school day morning I stand out in front of our school as some 500 or so young people stream in the doors. While greeting each of our kids I think about how different they are. Some love coming to school; some would rather have stayed in bed. There are those whose homes are intact and who slept soundly in a warm bed; others who have moved from home to home and are not sure where their next bed will be. Athletes, computer wizards, the socially adept and the painfully shy, students of all colors, sizes, shapes, and abilities walk through our doors and are, I hope, welcomed for who they are.

The challenge that the American high school faces today is how to meet the needs of these diverse learners in an era of standards and standardization. Believing that school improvement will come from fiat and edict, our schools are now measured not by how they create the conditions for every child to learn, but instead by how students score on standardized, fill-in-the-bubble exams that tell us little, if anything, about what they have learned or what they can do.

I think about this contradiction every day: how we are to treat students as individual learners while we only measure our effectiveness via standardized measures. Let me be clear, I am not against standards or accountability. But when we narrow what we are accountable for to only scores on standardized tests we will struggle to personalize the education we give each child.

And personalization is vital if we are to reach our students. This has always been the case. We have always personalized education—the question is who benefits from the personalized structures in our schools? If it is just students with some specialized and valued talent, then personalization will be limited to students who come with academic or artistic gifts easily spotted by the school.

The school play, the choir, the sports teams, the clubs—they all personalize school, for some students. The challenge is to turn our attention to the personalization of the entire school academic experience for *each and every student* so that every child in our care feels valued and thus is willing to work at what the school has to offer.

The schools described in this volume take on the challenge of personalization, often in the face of standardization, which does not serve their mission. Each one has demonstrated the ability to reach and engage students from all sectors of life in our United States. And each one has lessons to teach those of us who take seriously the challenge of personalizing education for our students. These schools are not unique; the work they have done with advisories, learning plans, curriculum and instruction, assessment, and leadership is shared by many schools in this nation. And if policymakers in this country were serious about promoting school improvement, they would pay attention to all the important work going on in schools like this. But perhaps that is too much for which to hope.

In the meantime, while we wait for policy to catch up with reality, we can learn from one another. Joe DiMartino and Denise Wolk give us that chance, letting each of the schools in this volume speak for themselves so we learn from our colleagues what really works when it comes to personalization in the name of higher standards for all students. Each story is inspirational, each one gave me yet another idea about how to meet the needs of the kids who will walk in the door tomorrow. And each school reminded me that if you want to do this work well, you have to, as Richard Esparza puts it in the first chapter, "have a belief [in our students] so strong that nothing will make it waver."

GEORGE H. WOOD
Principal, Federal Hocking Middle and High School
Executive Director, The Forum for Education and Democracy

There is a growing body of research that supports the continued development of personalized high schools as part of an overall portfolio of schools in cities and towns in the United States. In this Preface we examine a few examples from the research that supports the work described in the chapters that follow.

Developing Shared Values

The small schools movement has demonstrated to us that size alone is not the only condition for a successful school or small learning community (SLC). Other conditions include personalizing the environment so that students and teachers know each other well, establishing a unified vision of teaching and learning that binds the school and wider community, and the school's having the autonomy to create unified learning communities. Creating opportunities for teachers to serve in leadership positions through activities such as participating in design teams, conducting research as members of professional learning communities, and participating in shared-governance committees is an important way not only to promote a high school reform agenda, but also to develop a next wave of school leaders (NASSP, 2004).

In order for reform efforts to be successful it is vital not only that the members of the immediate school community share a common sense of purpose and shared vision, but also that the school receive the support of the district and school board to achieve their goals. John Clarke (2000) reveals the importance of building the conditions for systemic change: "Change can begin with the teacher, students, or the district, but you need the whole system to change to make it lasting." Public engagement can empower the school to solicit enduring support for change by creating key stakeholders in the process within district and school board leadership, as well as within the wider community outside the school walls. By engaging students, teachers, parents, community members, and political leaders the conditions for sustainable change can be created, but it takes time and continuous effort to keep the various constituencies engaged and to move people from being participants to becoming truly invested stakeholders in a process that has no real end. We have often asked leaders who have led school change efforts, "When were you finished?" and all of them answered "Not yet"— which is indicative of the fact that as the educational needs of students change throughout the years, schools must also change to meet those needs.

Creating an Environment That Fosters Independent Learning

Real-world experiences empower and inspire students to take control of their own learning. Schools with an innovative curriculum can create the conditions to allow for the use of Personal Learning and Postsecondary Plans (PLPPs), student-led conferences, project-based learning, service learning, and other innovative strategies to promote active students' engagement in their education (DiMartino & Clarke, 2008). Alternative forms of assessment can be used to gauge what a student knows and is able to do. Using student exhibitions and portfolios is a powerful alternative to standardized testing to gather how much depth a student has obtained in a subject area (Cushman-Brandjes, 2003; Levine, 2001). Programs such as Expeditionary Learning Outward Bound (ELOB) provide students with the opportunity to test their physical limits by learning skills such as team building and self-reliance while continuing academic growth in literacy, science, and math (Killion, 2000).

Listening to the students themselves can provide the school with a picture of what students' interests are, and how to design coursework around those interests (Park & Smith, 2003). Alternatives to traditional high schools, such as the Metropolitan Career and Technical Center (The Met) in Providence, Rhode Island, allow students to design their entire learning plan around their interests and gain real-world experience through projects that include internships in their interest area. This kind of learning experience can be a powerful incentive for students who are disengaged with traditional methods of teaching and learning (Grabelle & Littky, 2004). My own son graduated from The Met in June 2008 with his high school diploma and multiple certificates in welding as a result of his experience in this kind of hands-on learning. I am certain that without that kind of multisensory engagement he might have dropped out of school altogether (as did many of his peers in our upper-middle-class New England town).

Education Resource Strategies is a nonprofit organization that works closely with leaders of urban public school systems to rethink the use of district and school-level resources, supporting strategies for improved instruction and performance. A recent study by ERS reveals that smart uses of people, time, and money is critical to high student performance. *Strategic Designs: Lessons from Leading Edge Small Urban High Schools* demonstrates that innovative small schools are often more cost effective than the large comprehensive high schools they have replaced.

Adapting School Organization to Promote Student Success

Successful small schools and SLCs allow for flexibility in the leadership roles of teachers, staff, and administrators in which shared decision making becomes the norm. In this new paradigm the principal acts as an instructional leader rather than simply a building manager, thus creating an environment that encourages outside-of-the-box strategies to engage students and ultimately greater student achievement. Balancing teaching and learning issues with new school design and structures is critical to the success of new small schools and SLCs.

Creating new systems within the school, including the use of teacher teams, student advisory programs, personal learning plans, project based learning, peer mentoring, service learning programs, and more are all innovative methods for promoting student achievement while creating smaller and more personalized environments for students (DiMartino, Clarke, & Wolk, 2003). Working within these new organizational norms can be a daunting task for teachers and administrators, but learning new ways to use data and creating new organizational structures to support personalization is critical to success (DiMartino and Clarke, 2008; Schmoker, 1999). Adapting the schedule to work within emerging small learning communities is another key component to their success. There are a variety of strategies available to schools to adapt scheduling to suit their needs, and it is important to have structured conversations around what the new schedule(s) for the school should be.

Changes to school structures and organization are important steps for creating more personalized learning environments, but the more difficult shifts are those that involve the culture of the school. There must also be a focus on how teaching and learning occur in these new structures in order to capitalize on the investments made in structural reforms (Atkinson, French, and Rugen 2007). The new 3 Rs— relationships, relevance, and rigor—became driving principles behind the goals of promoting higher graduation rates and more equitable opportunities for students. Core strategies to improve academic performance and increase graduation rates have stressed offering more rigorous course work for all students, creating more real world learning applications, allowing for more exposure and exploration of possible career pathways, promoting stronger student-teacher relationships, and enabling a more personalized learning environment. One of the pitfalls for new and redesigned schools is they have often replicated the bad habits of their big siblings: too much tracking, too little inspired instruction and too few engaging classes, unequal access to comprehensive guidance and postsecondary planning, not enough early interventions and supports for students who struggle academi- cally, and inadequate services for students at risk or in crisis (Lieber, 2009). As you will read in the chapters that follow, by being mindful of all of these elements, the promise of personalized learning environments can and is being fulfilled.

The challenge of leading change in a school requires leaders who have the ability to focus not only on the specific initiatives to be implemented, but also on the ability to use influence to gain staff buy-in. The National Association of Secondary School Principals (NASSP) has pointed out the importance of focus- ing on school culture; in addition to focusing on the "what" of the change, lead- ers need to focus on the "how" of bringing change to school culture that will be sustained. They also stress the need for school teams to "gather data, explore possible solutions, assess readiness, create a plan, implement the plan as well as monitor and adjust the plan" (NASSP, 2009).

Standards-Based Teaching and Learning for Student Achievement

Standards-based instruction in any content area should be designed to establish what students should learn at each grade level. Standards should be more than just curriculum frameworks. They should lay out the skills, concepts, and knowledge that are achievable to build criteria for assessments and establish goals for learning. Standards should provide educational communities in each state with expected outcomes by grade level. With the ever-increasing pressure placed upon schools to demonstrate student achievement through scores on standardized and often high-stakes tests, the need for standards-based instruction is greater than ever. As Carol Ann Tomlinson said, " . . . standards-based instruction and the high-stakes testing that drives it can often feel like a locomotive rolling over everything in its path, including individualized learning" (Tomlinson, 2001), and it is easy for the testing juggernaut to overtake the underlying importance of creating a curriculum that is aligned to clearly defined standards. The trick is in knowing how to achieve academic rigor while providing a variety of ways for students to engage with the curriculum so they can see its relevance in their lives or future aspirations.

Small schools and SLCs can use a variety of strategies for addressing this challenge. Teachers can team-teach, use differentiated instruction techniques, and integrate content across the discipline areas to offer support to increase student achievement (Callahan & Ryan, 2003). The integration of math and humanities, for example, can help teachers transform their practice to provide more meaningful and productive experiences for students (Worsley, 2003). Building adolescent literacy skills is a powerful means for students to achieve competency, and research supports the commonsense notion that time spent reading and writing will help students improve those skills (Davidson & Koppenhaver, 1993). The research also supports the use of the writing process as an integral part of content-area literacy development (Alvermann & others, 1998; Cotton, 1988; Langer, 2001). Using project-based instruction is another excellent way to integrate various skills across the content areas (see Chapters Three, Four, and Five for examples of this).

Veteran school researcher and reformer Linda Darling-Hammond (2005) underscores the underlying need for standards-based teaching and learning: "We're talking about the kind of education that a small number of folks have had access to for over a hundred years and making that available to a much larger number of students, in fact all students. It's not a passing fad or fancy. It's really inventing schools for the twenty-first century that enable our society to continue to be the kind of democratic and highly productive society that it's been."

DENISE L. WOLK

Bibliography

Atkinson, M., French, D., & Rugen, L. (2007). *Creating small schools: A handbook for raising equity and achievement.* Thousand Oaks, CA: Corwin Press.

Alvermann, D. E., Hinchman, K. A., Moore, D. W., Phelps, S. F., & Waff, D. R. (Eds.). (1998). *Reconceptualizing the literacies in adolescents' lives.* Mahwah, NJ: Erlbaum.

Block scheduling: Innovations with time. (1998). Providence, RI: The Education Alliance/LAB at Brown University.

Callahan, J., & Ryan, L. (2003). Service-learning: One strategy to meet beginning teacher standards. *Generator.* St. Paul, MN: National Youth Leadership Council.

Clarke, J. (2000). *Dynamics of change in high school teaching: A study of Innovation in five Vermont professional development schools.* , Providence, RI: The Education Alliance/LAB at Brown University.

Cotton, K. (1988). *Instructional reinforcement. Close-up No. 3.* Portland, OR: Northwest Regional Educational Laboratory.

Cushman-Brandjes, E. (2003). Assessing to engage: Developing personal profiles for each student ch. 2 in *Personalized learning: Preparing high school students to create their futures.* Lanham, MD: Scarecrow Press.

Darling-Hammond, L., & Bransford, R. (2005). *Preparing teachers for a changing world: What teachers should learn and be able to do.* San Francisco: Jossey-Bass.

Davidson, J., & Koppenhaver, D. (1993). *Adolescent literacy: What works and why.* Hamden, CT: Garland Publishing, Inc.

DiMartino, J., & Clarke, J. (2008). *Personalizing the high school experience for each student.* Alexandria, VA: ASCD.

DiMartino, J., Clarke, J., & Wolk, D. (Eds.) (2003). *Personalized learning: Preparing high school students to create their futures.* Lanham, MD: Scarecrow Press.

Grabelle, S., & Littky, D. (2004). *The big picture: Education is everyone's business.* Richmond, VA: ASCD.

Killion, J. (2000). *What works in the middle: Results-based staff development.* Washington, DC: NSDC.

Langer, J. A. (2001). *Guidelines for teaching middle and high school students to read and write well.* Albany, NY: National Research Center on English Learning and Achievement, State University of New York at Albany.

Levine, E. (2001). *The big picture: Big lessons from a small school.* New York: Teachers College Press.

Lieber, C. (2009). *Making learning REAL: Reaching and engaging all learners in secondary classrooms.* Cambridge, MA: Educators for Social Responsibility.

National Association of Secondary School Principals. (2004). *Breaking Ranks II: Strategies for leading high school reform.* Reston, VA: NASSP.

National Association of Secondary School Principals. (2009). *Breaking ranks a Field Guide for Leading Change.* Reston, VA: NASSP.

Park, J., & Smith, P. (2003). *Turn up the volume. Principal Leadership, 3*(6), 37–41. Reston, VA: NASSP.

Schmoker, M. (1999). *Results: The key to continuous school improvement,* 2nd ed. Richmond, VA: ASCD.

Shields, R., & Hawley Miles, K. (2008). *Strategic designs: Lessons from leading edge small urban high schools.* Cambridge, MA: Education Resource Strategies.

Teachers College Record (2004), *106* (6), 1047–1085. http://www.tcrecord.org

Tomlinson, C. (2001). Standards and the art of teaching: Crafting high-quality classrooms. *NASSP Bulletin, 85*(622), 38–47.

Worsley, D. (2003). *Changing systems to personalize learning: Teaching to each student.* Providence, RI: The Education Alliance at Brown University.

INTRODUCTION

The American high school is under siege. High school educators are being bombarded daily with evidence of how poorly our adolescents fare in international comparisons of secondary schooling.

To be honest, the evidence that other nations are better equipping their populace for the twenty-first century world is quite compelling. According to the Organization for Economic Cooperation and Development, an organization of 30 industrialized nations (the members of which do not include India and China, our two major economic competitors), the percentage of our populace that is completing high school has dropped from the first to eighteenth place. The United States also no longer leads the world in the percentage of population holding a bachelor's degree, having been surpassed by a number of nations, including South Korea, where half of its youth are earning college degrees although only 20% of their population graduated from high school a generation ago. The PISA (Programme of International Student Assessment) exam, which is administered to 15-year-olds in OECD (Organisation for Economic Co-operation and Development) countries, shows that our scores have fallen behind 20 other countries in math and science. Achieve, Inc., a bipartisan, nonprofit organization that helps states raise academic standards, improve assessments, and strengthen accountability to prepare all young people for postsecondary education, work, and citizenship, conducted the American Diploma Project study in 2003 and came to the inescapable conclusion that the skills necessary to be successful in entry level manufacturing positions are the same as the skills necessary to be successful in the freshman year of college.

National data gathered by Achieve show that for every 100 students who enter the ninth grade, only 68 graduate from high school four years later. Of the original 100 only 40 return for their second year of college and only 18 graduate from college ten years after entering the ninth grade. Unfortunately, according to the National Center on Education and the Economy, 32% of the jobs held by 30- to 60-year-olds in this country are filled by individuals with a bachelor's degree or higher. This results in a skills gap that is huge. As the 32% that hold jobs requiring a bachelor's degree retire, we are only currently generating 18% of our population to fill those jobs! This presents a major economic problem for our country.

Although these statistics are pretty damning, besides preparing our citizenry for economic competitiveness as the world's foremost democracy, we need to prepare our youth to become full participants in a democratic society.

These data, although certainly depressing, are often used to cast aspersions on the educators who are struggling to educate our youth to high standards. This is indeed unfortunate when one considers that the basic design of the American high school was created in the nineteenth century and has not been significantly changed in more than a century. We are trying to educate our citizens in a high-speed age with horse and buggy methods. Our educational system was designed when at most 5% of American young men and virtually none of our young women attended high school. Now, thanks to tireless, determined efforts by our educators, we are educating one third of the students in our high schools to be successful in post secondary education. Clearly a remarkable feat! But despite all of these efforts, the results are no longer good enough. Frankly, meeting the new demands that are being placed on our high schools are unlikely to be met without major redesign of the entire secondary education system in this country.

The National High School Alliance, a partnership of nearly 50 organizations representing a diverse cross-section of perspectives and approaches sharing the commitment to promote excellence, equity, and development of high school–age youth, has agreed on a framework for the high school of the twenty-first century. The National High School Alliance (HAS) released their landmark *A Call to Action: Transforming High School for All Youth,* which provides leaders at the national, state, district, school, and community levels with a common framework for building public will, developing supportive policies, and actually implementing the practices needed to radically change the traditional, factory-model high school that tracks and sorts students. *A Call to Action* identified six core principles for student success:

- Personalized learning environments
- Academic engagement of all students
- Empowered educators
- Accountable leaders
- Engaged community and youth
- An integrated system of high standards, curriculum, instruction, assessments, and supports

The Personalized High School: Making Learning Count for Adolescents explores the real-world work of redesigning high school from the perspectives of high school change agents and students themselves. Schools from across the country are highlighted throughout this book to exemplify various strategies of high school reform that align with the goals of the *Call to Action*, including designing and using personalized learning plans and portfolios, allowing students to contribute to their own educational experiences through providing expanded opportunities for students' voices to inform and influence adults' decisions, and using authentic assessments including exhibitions for students to demonstrate what they know and are able to do.

The Personalized High School leads off with the story of how implementing a student/teacher advisory program designed to support every student by providing ties to adults in the building and connecting with families of the students made all the difference in a poverty-ridden town in rural Washington. Meanwhile, across the country in suburban Massachusetts, the teachers and administrators have been using and refining personal learning plans and portfolios to help students discover their interests and blaze their own trail to the future. In the wine country of California, students at New Technology High School engage in a wide variety of projects to stretch the limits of their learning. In the Midwest, teachers at Minnesota New Country School have formed a unique partnership to provide personalized learning environments for all students. In New York City, School of the Future has been using integrated assessments to go well beyond the bounds of standardized assessment, allowing urban students to demonstrate what they know and are able to do in a rich learning environment. The tough choices involved in making structural and cultural leadership changes are highlighted the story of San Diego's Madison High School. Back in New England, the principal and staff at Boston Arts Academy prove that by offering opportunities to form genuine and supportive professional learning communities, the whole school flourishes. Hands-on, experiential learning is a key component in the Big Picture approach to teaching and learning by giving students the opportunity to learn highly challenging material with significant personal relevance at Front Range Early College High School in Denver. Each of the chapters in this book provides a real-world example of how the critical elements of small schools are working for students across our nation.

JOSEPH A. DIMARTINO

THE PERSONALIZED
HIGH SCHOOL

PART ONE Personalizing Your School Environment

Advisories

Believe in Students First

Ricardo Leblanc-Esparza

Granger High School, Granger, Washington

There are two things you notice about Richard Esparza right away: he smiles contagiously, and he wavers not a bit. Those traits have gone a long way toward helping him transform Granger High School over the past eight years, raising the school from the lowest-performing school in the state when he arrived as principal in 1999 to one of the highest-performing schools in 2006. Facing challenges that many perceive as obstacles to learning—high poverty, minority, crime, and dropout rates, and low reading levels, test scores, and student engagement—Richard Esparza has been undeterred, determined that the students could achieve, and resolved not to lose a single one. Convinced that the strategies for creating a manageable system at Granger can work anywhere, he shares the story of his school's remarkable turnaround.

I live in a high-poverty, migrant community where, for some students in my school, 13 people live in a house, another two live in an outside trailer, the mom lives in another trailer, and a student sorts bitterroots in the living room where he sleeps with his cousin.

This community in Granger, Washington, leads to some challenging demographics in Granger High School: 90% free and reduced lunch, 21% migrant, 32% bilingual, and 90% students of color—and these are all excuses that people gave as reasons the kids here couldn't learn. What do you think our school was like? Do you think we had gang problems? Do you think we had kids smoking pot in the bathrooms and in the bushes? Yes, yes, and yes. Plus we had low expectations from students, staff, and even parents. All of those things were in place. Some will say it's about color and poverty, but poverty is what cuts across all races—it's the biggest indicator across the board to determine whether a school will be successful or not. When I came to Granger High in the spring of 1999, our school had the highest reported crime rate in the state of Washington, our test scores were among the lowest in the state, and we had a dismal 58% graduation rate.

We realized that to see improvements in these areas we would have to change our system to push students to experience success and not lose students by focusing on three basic principles:

1. Make sure students are attending school
2. Make sure they are getting good grades
3. Help them find a career path or career goals

The key was to find a way that would let us track attendance and grades closely, and help us guide students to discover their own passions and interests. We needed a system that promoted a personal connection to the students, something that offered a manageable ratio of students to adults, that involved parents and caregivers, and that helped students engage with the school and their education. In short, we needed a revolution in our high school.

Break It Down

The reality is that in the public school system, the numbers often do not make it feasible for us to truly catch all the students, particularly those in danger of dropping out. For example, when I started at Granger, the student to counselor ratio was 400:1 and teachers saw 140 students a day.

Think about it: if there are 400 students to one counselor, what happens when the student goes to get help from that counselor? Sometimes they're out to lunch. Other times they're working with an academically proficient student, or a pregnant student, or a struggling student. In the beginning my more proficient students were frustrated with the counselors, saying things like, "Mr. Esparza, they're always working with the pregnant girls, or the drug abuse kids, the counselor is always tied up and we never can get the academic support we need." On the other side, there were the lost kids who often didn't have enough courage to go see the counselor, or if they did finally get up the courage, saw that the counselors were tied up doing something else.

How many times would a student get turned away before finally giving up?

Our traditional education system is built around managing too many students. It's impossible to know them well, to carefully track their progress, or to help them identify their interests. Students need someone to pay attention, offer encouragement, convince them that their presence at the school is important, and believe in their potential. If you were to say to a coach—could you coach 400 kids and really get to know them and help them be successful? What do you think that coach would tell you? It's just not doable. So what's the answer?

You have to break down the system into manageable numbers.

20:1 Advisories Work

I often hear, "Gosh, that's not doable, we're a very, very large school." When you look at our whole state of Washington and see the certificated staff to student ratio, it's about a 20:1 ratio across the board if you include the librarians and administrators. So can our systems truly be broken down? The numbers say yes, it is possible.

I hadn't done advisories before. It was a leap of faith but something I was willing to try, since Granger had the lowest academic performance in the state when I arrived: 11% writing, 20% reading, and 4% math.

To begin with, we had a 15-minute time period set aside for Channel 1, and 15 minutes for silent, sustained reading. I tried to negotiate with Channel 1 for bigger TVs. Kids try to be cool and won't wear glasses but then they can't see the TV. I didn't get the larger TVs, so I decided in that first year to use those 30 minutes for students to engage in reading instead, and allow for teachers to do paperwork. I kept thinking about what else we could do for our students during this 30-minute period.

During the second year, I learned that my staff didn't know what it takes for students to graduate. I realized that if we were to break this system down, how much more powerful it could be if we each took care of students as if they were our own kids, be quasi-parents. And if you don't have kids, then you'd take care of them the way you would have wanted to be treated.

I explained to my staff that this was only going to help them. In a high-poverty, high-failing school, if 40% of students are failing, that means 40 out of 100 students are failing—40 kids that you are supposed to connect with to make it work for them. If you break the system down further, every adult has eight students instead of 40. It's unlikely that you are going to connect with 40 students, but it's a lot more realistic to expect it to happen if you have five or eight in an advisory group to try to find a way to light their fire. Everyone can work five at-risk students in addition to their top students, middle students, and lesson planning. It's still a challenge, but the smaller numbers makes sense.

I hired an instructional facilitator to do all the leg work for creating advisories—the advisors don't even have to make copies. We are using Navigation 101, a curriculum designed to help students with job shadows, career goals, interest inventory, college statement, and so forth, under the basic philosophy that encourages students to attend school, get good grades, and define a career goal. Undeclared majors are OK, because remember how hard it was to figure out what you wanted to do for a job? But you need to be able to read, write, and do the math at or above your grade level.

I had my first group of advisees with me for two years, sharing an advisory with a counselor. In trying to figure out how to make this work, we made the mistake of selecting all at-risk kids, which led to a *Welcome Back Kotter* group of kids. The kids would feed off each other. There was also no continuity—with two days with the counselor as advisor, and two days with me. I'd hear, "Ms. Bush said we could do this, this, and this."

We also experienced the opposite extreme—one teacher convinced me to let him have all FFA (Future Farmers of America) students, who pretty much rested on their laurels and became an elitist club.

We realized that we needed to balance advisory groups by reading level: fourth and fifth grade level readers with ninth and tenth grade level readers. That way kids can see role models of studious peers. The expectation is that they are going to raise their skill level. And like professional sports teams, we need to allow people to be traded. If you're not getting along, if personalities don't match, it's OK to change within grade level advisories.

This system won't work meeting only twice a year or once a month. Advisory classes at our school meet Monday, Tuesday, Thursday, and Friday, each focusing on specific content, for example reading, math, portfolio development, homework, or special topics.

Teachers give all the mentors/advisors progress reports every other Friday. I am working with five at-risk students. With every mentor taking care of five at-risk students, now you're talking about a system that's truly going to be able to keep track of kids. That's a doable system. *Five.* If I had 50, plus the other 100 students I'm supposed to take care of, it's just too much. That's what we're expecting our educators to do, and that's why we're losing the kids in the shuffle.

I expect my advisors/mentors to contact and take care of their 20 kids as if they're their own. So they are the ones who are going to contact the parents, letting them know that so and so is not getting the job done.

We don't lose kids anymore. We know who has problems with depression, drugs/alcohol, their boyfriend/girlfriend, or who is pregnant. OK, you're smoking pot—that's not good. One student showed up under the influence of marijuana to a parent conference. The message was, *"You are busted. You're going to the drug/alcohol counselor."* One year at the prom, one of the seniors had a miscarriage on the way to the prom. As awful as it was for her, is that a student we were going to lose? No, my counselor was available to follow up with her. Her advisor would know and be able to support her. Our thinking is: if kids have problems you can't solve, what do you do as a parent? Don't you refer them to a specialist? We do the same as advisors.

I have 18 advisees this year that I've had since eighth grade, and they're all juniors now. All I've done is keep track of their attendance and their grades. I've

Our Goals for Advisory

1. Every student will be well-known, both personally and academically, by at least one adult staff member.

2. Every student will be pushed to increase their reading level and math level.

3. Every student will be challenged to meet rigorous academic standards in an appropriate educational program.

4. Every student will be provided with opportunities to experience the benefits of community membership and to develop and practice leadership.

5. Every student will be prepared for whatever he or she chooses to do after graduation, with a strong transcript, a career pathway, a plan, and a portfolio.

also helped them find a career goal. As much as I love them, they're getting to the age at which it's time to push them out of the nest. They're going to be 18, and they're going to graduate. They've gone on job shadows, tried to find the career they want, worked on reading skills or math skills, gotten their homework done or worked at establishing relationships during that advising time.

I think of the journey I've been on with so many of them—my job is taking care of my 18 kids, but I take care of all of them, and keep track of the data. At the sophomore class meeting, trying to be an advisor to all on a larger scale, I tell them about a poster I have in my office, called the Three Roads of Life. On it, there's a line that starts when you're born and ends when you die. In between, you're going to be on the road. The top road of life has good-to-great income (anything that has benefits). The average income road of life may have benefits, and can be a really dicey area at the end of your journey. The low income road of life (minimum wage, likely no benefits) is where 90% of our kids come from. I tell the students the kinds of grades that are attached to it: you have to get As, Bs, and Cs to be on the good-to-great road.

I don't make the rules of the system, but I do know how it works. I try to inspire them to take the top road of life. I know the kids we haven't captured because I see their grades, and their grades tell me everything.

Include the Parent or Caregiver

How about parents? How important are they? I'll ask you: Who helped you? Who helped you get to where you are? Maybe it wasn't a mom and dad but it was likely to be someone you lived with. Maybe you lived with grandparents or friends of the family, but somebody gave you that support.

As educators, we can't do this by ourselves. With 70% of a student's life spent away from school, if we don't make caregivers a part of this equation, we're missing a big part. (I say *caregiver* because in this high-poverty area, 25% of the students I see have a mom and dad at home. The rest are with their grandmother, friend of the family, aunt, uncle, sister, brother. They live with someone but more often than not it's not the mom and dad.)

When I started at Granger, the test scores showed that 10% of the students were reading at standard. *Ten percent.* And only 23% of parents were coming to conferences. The staff was happy with the 23%. When I asked why, I learned that it was because there had been 10% participation the previous year. Part of the problem was that conferences were being scheduled during the school day, and in a high-poverty area where parents don't have time off, if they don't work, they don't get paid. So we moved the conferences to the evenings and still only 25 parents out of 800 came in.

I looked at this statistic: 10% of kids were meeting standards at the same time that 10% of the parents were coming to conferences.

The turning point came during my first year as principal when a parent came to me in tears. First she was mad because her son was suspended, and I rarely suspend kids. But this kid deserved to be suspended. She told me, "Please let him back into school. I just want him to graduate, he's a senior." I looked up his credits—he had six credits to his name, PE and some vocational credits. I had to be the one to break the news to her and say, "I'm sorry, ma'am, your son only has six credits. We need 24 to graduate."

That's when the tears came and she said, "That's not possible. I have fed him breakfast. I have given him lunch money for four years. I need him to graduate. I don't have a husband at home. I need him to get a good job so he can help the family out." It wasn't possible. Six credits and here he was a senior and it was spring of his senior year.

That's when I made a commitment that we need to change our system, we need to connect with parents, we need to communicate because I never want to go through this again where I'm looking at a parent, having to break the news that there's no way their child is going to graduate on time. One way or the other we're going to get them to the conferences and it's going to be student-led. We do this by developing a team that *includes* the parent.

In the system we set up, each advisor meets 18 sets of caregivers. In the other system, a teacher would meet 150 × 2, or close to 300 parents, and think, "Am I really getting messages across?" Students now feel, "I really work hard because I don't want to have to explain to my parents why I'm not doing well at parent-teacher conferences."

I met the parents of my advisees in the spring of eighth grade year. It was amazing to hear some parents learn and be surprised. Family dynamics tend to be broken in a high-poverty school like mine. You have to roll up your sleeves and go into the good, bad, and ugly of life. I met them again freshman year, and with the personalized education plan, we meet twice a year and communicate in between. We send paper progress reports home every two weeks. If a parent contacts me and says, "My son isn't bringing progress reports home . . . can I come by and pick them up?" I respond, "No. That's your responsibility. . . . your end of the bargain." Sometimes you end up counseling parents to be parents.

I tell the parents about the Three Roads of Life, and ask them, "Where do you want your kids?" I commonly hear that they don't want their kids to have to do what they do. "I work hard so they have it easier."

Most of my parents don't have an education. They haven't gone to third or fourth grade. If they don't have an education, I have to educate them. I'm talking about starting with the basics—A, B, C, D, and F. One student had convinced his parents that F was good. I've trained my parents—a quarter is 45 days, a semester is 90 days, credits add up, A is great, B is OK, and so forth. This is where I came from. My own parents didn't have an education but they learned the difference between an A, B, C, D, and F. And once they knew that, that was it, they held us to that standard. We send a monthly calendar in the mail and tell the parents to be looking for it. I love this system.

For the eighth time now, 100% of caregivers have attended conferences— whoever is there—foster parent, friends, or relatives. I will accept no less than 100% of our parents. Teachers are proud of the fact that we've got 100% participation. They compete with each other to see who can get the most participants.

Believe in the Students

We believe that all students can achieve. We have learned that students who come to high school with low academic skills can achieve. People often place blame on why students don't achieve. In elementary school they blame the parent, in middle school they blame the elementary school, and in high school they blame the middle school. But regardless of why, some students arrive at high school with low academic skills. What can you do about it? You have to start with the premise that even though they've come with low academic skills, it doesn't mean that they can't change in the high school.

I believe in Maslow's Hierarchy of Needs. If the most basic needs of food, shelter, safety, and support are met, and the personal need for love and belonging is met, it's amazing what students can do. If students feel somebody truly cares about them and is going to push them to get through school, they can and do rise to meet our expectations.

One way we support students in their learning is through the Personalized Education Plan (PEP). In our state, any student who did not meet standards in seventh grade is required to develop a student learning plan. In my view, every student needs a plan.

The PEP is very basic. The idea is to allow students to sit down in a private setting with an adult to guide them and review their educational progress to date. It is important that students recognize that it is their education and their future. The PEP centers around reading scores, math scores, and requires students to identify a career goal. It's a short, simple agreement between the student and the caregiver. It's not a hard plan. It asks students, "What do you agree to do for your future?" It also asks adults to identify what they agree to do as a support person. I am the support person, and the parent.

Data are an important part of the PEP. In the student-led conferences, you can see the student's current grade level in reading and math, and the expectation is that he or she is at or above grade level. Students take the WASL (Washington Assessment of Student Learning), a state assessment during sophomore year, and have to meet that standard. I have all students at Granger High take the ASVAB (Armed Services Vocational Aptitude Battery) as juniors, explaining to them that this is an assessment that is part of the real world.

Students need to know what their skill level is in order to get better. By exposing them to real expectations, they understand what they need to know and can develop strategies for improving any areas necessary. We have English teachers available before school, math teachers after school, and teachers available during lunch. By knowing what their level is, students are motivated to show up and seek extra help.

How do we keep high expectations? We changed our mission statement. It now reads, "*All students will be expected to reach . . .*" Formerly, it was: "*All students will be given the opportunity . . .*" It took all the responsibility off us and gave it to the students, and they could choose to take it or not. Now students know that we expect them to be successful, and we're going to contact the parents if they're not getting the job done.

We have implemented a referral program so that any student who falls below a C is referred to the academic success program before or after school or during lunch break, or both. In order to exit out of this program, students must achieve a C or better.

Since I came to Granger High in Spring 1999, we've gone from being the school with the highest reported crime rate in the state of Washington to the one with the lowest reported crime rate. At the same time, test scores went from the lowest to the highest, and we went from a 58% graduation rate to a 90% graduation rate in 2006.

The national dropout statistics haven't really changed since the 1970s. The graduation rate nationwide for African American, Latino, and Native American students is 50% or less. Comparing the lowest income quartile to the highest, the dropout rate goes up six times. This is unacceptable. We need to operate school like a business. In a business, if you were only producing 30% of products that work, you'd be out of business. Even 60 or 70% would not do. That's what I'm looking at. I'm not happy with 90%. That means our system didn't work for 10% of the students. I have pictures of people on my wall, every percentage is represented by faces—those are the people who are going out in society, either to improve society or to be lost souls mired in a cycle of poverty that never ends.

Lessons Learned

The only way we truly save this world is one person at a time. At Granger High, we're experiencing a whole system that is working for students, and I've seen that it is all so doable. Here are some lessons we've learned along the way that may help other school systems in their efforts to connect with and not lose students:

- You have to believe in students in order for them to believe in themselves.

- Know your clients. Understand the cultural influences on parents when you're trying to connect with them; that's what successful businesses do. For example, in some Hispanic cultures the traditional handshake is rude and confrontational and should begin more informally by asking questions like, "How are you doing? How's the family? How are the kids? Or "Let's have Rodrigo tell us how he's doing." Learn your cultures and understand who you serve. That way parents and other caregivers will feel more welcome.

- Learn from your neighbor. Don't recreate the wheel—visit and learn from places that are being successful. It's like sports—when another team has won 18 times and lost twice and my program has lost 18 times and won twice, I want to know how that team is doing it. Find a place that has already done the kind of work that you're considering and learn from them. People are willing to share.

- Prepare and train your staff. Provide the time. You can't just say, "Read this and let's get to it." Create ways for staff to collaborate. At Granger High, we have early release every Wednesday, a two-hour block of time to work together consistently. Before committing to this schedule, it was once a month for three hours, but then professional development became like a flavor of the month. Have a systemic approach to staff development, pulling time out of the school day to get it done so it pays off for staff and students.

- Expose students to a different reality. In larger towns and cities when students live in the middle class or above, they understand that you have to have money, and they have awareness of what is going on in the world around them. Most students here haven't been far from a small town and believe this is what reality is. We take them on field trips, for example, to an Idaho theme park as a reward instead of senior skip day and open their eyes to possibilities beyond their own small town.

- Allow kids to try, try again. Promote retesting, as most real world exams permit a retake, for example driving tests, bar exams, SATs, and so on. At the prom recently, one of the kids in her prom dress said, "Ms. Cartwright, don't forget I'm going to retake that test." We expect students to learn the material, and sometimes it just takes time to get it all down, so allowing students multiple opportunities to demonstrate their learning provides that extra push they need to ensure future success and sustained effort.

- Break down the negative belief system. People have a hard time looking at themselves—they've tried their hardest, done everything they can, and some kids still fail. Students will think they're failures if we let them, and it creates a cycle of failure until you show them a different way. With the right support, students can reach a standard. Build that up. Maybe the system wasn't establishing a relationship or connection with the kids, but adults can reshape the system—we can create connections and build relationships with students to help meet their needs and reshape those negative beliefs.

- To convince your staff, do the research. It's all about the *BFOs*: the Blinding Flashes of the Obvious. When we broke down the numbers I asked my staff, "Guys, do you want to take care of five at-risk kids as an advisor and try to get them to succeed?" We all knew that we weren't reaching the larger number of 40–50 at-risk students, and academic teachers see between 140 and 180 students a day. When we broke down the numbers and showed them that it really was possible, teachers really connected with that one.

- Celebrate the successes and make the celebrations public. Some people don't believe it can be done because they haven't seen a high school like Granger be successful. I'm here to tell you, "It's being done, academic success is happening in unexpected schools." "*Si puede.*" "Yes it can be done." People who have doubts begin to believe after they start seeing the results.
- Have fun, and get it done at the same time.

It boils downs to this: you have to have a belief so strong that nothing will make it waver. For me, I was fortunate that I grew up in a life of poverty, part of a migrant family with 10 people in the house, and at the tail end of moving around. I went to three schools, ending up in the school 20 miles down the road from where I am now. When I see kids who are migrants, kids of color, I look at myself as not being different from any of them and I think, "How can I get my students to do what I've done?" I never would waver from the basic belief that all students truly can reach their academic and social potential, but it's a paradigm shift for many. I never had a paradigm shift—for me it's exciting and awesome to see it happen. It's also very satisfying to know how many of our students are going to graduate and go on to college, breaking the cycle of poverty and creating ripple effects in their family for generations to come.

Reflection Questions

1. What do the data at your school tell you about student engagement?
2. Does your school have an advisory program in place?
   a. If so, how do you know it is effective? Is there a plan for continuous assessment and adjustments to meet the ongoing needs of students?
   b. Is your advisory program used simply for community building and development of social skills, or does it provide support for students' academic growth and college-exploration activities?
   c. If not, how could implementing an advisory program benefit students in your school?
   d. How would your school organize the planning and implementation activities involved in creating and sustaining a high-quality advisory program for all students?

3. Is there a group within the school that can take responsibility for continuous development and growth of the advisory program? How can students be involved in advisory development?

4. How will or does your school provide ongoing professional development for advisors?

Resources

The Advisory Library. Educators for Social Responsibility, www.esrnational.org Sixteen books full of activities and resources that can be used in advisory plus a handbook with tips for how to use the books.

DiMartino, J., & Clarke, J. (2008). *The Heart of School Principal Leadership*, 9(3). Reston, VA: NASSP.

DiMartino, J., & Clarke, J. (2008). *Personalizing the High School Experience for Each Student.* Alexandria, VA: ASCD.

DiMartino, J., Clarke, J., & Wolk, D. (eds.) (2003). *Personalized Learning: Preparing High School Students to Create their Futures.* Lanham, MD: Rowman & Littlefield.

DiMartino, J., Mangiante, E., & Miles, S. (2006). *High Schools at Work: Creating Student-Centered Learning.* (DVDs with facilitator's guide) Alexandria, VA: ASCD.

Educators for Social Responsibility, www.esrnational.org

Osofsky, D., Sinner, G., & Wolk, D. (2003). *Changing Systems to Personalize Learning: Discover the Power of Advisories,* Providence, RI: Northeast and Islands Regional Educational Laboratory. Download at http://www.alliance.brown.edu/db/ea_catalog.php

Poliner, R., & Lieber, C. M. (2004). *The Advisory Guide: Designing and Implementing Effective Advisory Programs in Secondary Schools.* Cambridge, MA: Educators for Social Responsibility.

Personal Learning Plans

Making It Personal to Engage Students

Debbie Osofsky and Teri Schrader

Francis W. Parker Charter Essential School, Devens, Massachusetts

What if . . . ? Asking Essential Questions

What if every student was able to articulate two or three goals for the school year and was mindful and reflective of her progress towards them?

What if you knew as a teacher the goals held in common among the students you teach and could tailor your curriculum, instruction, and assessment accordingly so as to best meet their needs?

What if there was a process in place in your school that provided structure, support, and a means to involve all parents, students, and teachers in student learning and growth?

What if?

With this very question in mind, The Francis W. Parker Charter Essential School opened its doors in September of 1995 after a year of planning by its founders and prospective members of the community. The school began with 120 students in grades seven and eight and now, 12 years later, enrolls 368 students in grades seven through twelve. Our school is located in North Central Massachusetts, in a sprawling region of suburbs, rural towns, and a few small cities. As we set out to create the school, many parents eagerly joined the growing conversation about what it would mean not only to send their children forward into an experiment but to take part in its creation. Parents laid bare their deepest hopes for their children and shared their disappointment about the ways their children were "doing school" and what school seemed to be doing to their children. They lamented that their children were increasingly going through the motions, their growing sense that they were not known well at school, and that the goals and priorities for learning seemed to be drifting farther and farther away from their children and themselves, and ever closer to standards set by others, elsewhere. What was lacking was the opportunity for students, parents, and teachers to collaboratively craft an educational experience that made sense for each individual child.

A Student Perspective: Emily's Story

I stared blankly at the piece of paper entitled "Emily Browning's Personal Learning Plan." I was just a little seventh grader trying to do well in school, why was I being asked to do this? At my old school I was never asked to reflect on my own learning. I was getting good grades and that's all that seemed to matter. Now I was being asked to do the very thing I hated the most: talking to others about myself. In my first conference I was like a locked box; nothing was going to pry me open.

I'll admit my experience with PLPs my first year at Parker was frightening and something I dreaded, but over time I could see how the process was contributing to my learning and my growth as a person.

Throughout my experience as a student at Parker, I struggled with speaking up in the classroom. Although I was a good student and performed well on written assignments, I hardly ever shared my thoughts in class. Every year I set the same goal: to participate more in class. My advisor and I developed strategies such as asking questions when I am confused, raising my hand whenever I have something to say instead of overanalyzing my thoughts, writing notes in advance to prepare for class discussions, and practicing talking in small groups in order to become more comfortable speaking in larger groups. My teachers tried to help me with my goal in various ways, like calling on me even if I hadn't raised my hand, or congratulating me at the end of class if I had contributed to class discussion. Gradually, I made progress. In my freshman year in college, I found myself slipping back into my old habits. When I recognized this, I thought back to

---

past strategies I had employed in high school and used them again to participate more in my college classes.

The PLP process forced me to become organized and recognize what I needed to accomplish in order to reach my personal goals. Each year, the process became easier for me and was no longer something I feared. As I grew older, I was encouraged to move beyond academic goals and create some personal ones as well. My advisors and teachers let me know that academics were not all that mattered, that pursuing other interests and goals outside of the academic setting were equally important. These goals varied throughout the years: improve my shot in basketball, learn the guitar, get involved in community service, and, when senior year approached, begin the process of applying to college.

Throughout my years at Parker, I learned the skills I needed to critically analyze how I was doing in school, to set my own goals according to my own learning style, and to take responsibility for my own learning. Instead of the teacher just telling me what I needed to work on, I was given my own personal time to think and reflect on my own goals and strategies. My advisor was always there to tell me when I was being unreasonable or to make suggestions for ways to work on my goals. The PLP process allowed me to develop close and meaningful relationships with teachers with whom I could feel comfortable confiding. They really got to know me—my strengths as well as my weaknesses.

The skills I developed from going through the PLP process every year at Parker have served me well since graduation from high school. In college, I am not required to fill out a yearly personal learning plan, but I have some skills now that enable me to identify my strengths and weaknesses and to personally create goals and strategies to help me accomplish them. Several times, I have contacted Parker teachers with whom I developed especially close relationships to ask for their guidance. The strange habits I was asked to cultivate as a seventh grader are second nature to me now.

Emily Browning graduated from Parker in 2005. She is currently a student at Macalester College in St. Paul, MN, where she is majoring in Anthropology. She enjoys traveling, sports, and working with children.

A Coalition School

What emerged from this dialogue was the creation of a school that fully embodies the Ten Common Principles of the Coalition of Essential Schools, where knowing our students well allows us to participate fully, caringly, and tirelessly in the commitment to teach in a manner that we believe will open students to new ideas, challenge their intellect, and help them find resilience, courage, and their best version of themselves. In every way that matters, Parker benefits from this strong foundation in the Ten Common Principles. They are the basis for the school's charter, providing guidance for every aspect of the life of the school from how we structure our academic program to the ways in which we foster professional development among the staff to the ways in which we deliberately nurture the relationships that shape our community.

The Ten Common Principles of the Coalition of Essential Schools

1. The school should focus on helping adolescents learn to use their minds well.

2. The school's goals should be simple: that each student master a limited number of essential skills and areas of knowledge.

3. The school's goals should apply to all students, while the means to these goals will vary as those students themselves vary.

4. Teaching and learning should be personalized to the maximum feasible extent.

5. The governing practical metaphor of the school should be student as worker rather than the more familiar metaphor of teacher as deliverer of instructional services.

6. Teaching and learning should be documented and assessed with tools based on student performance of real tasks.

7. The tone of the school should explicitly and self-consciously stress values of unanxious expectation ("I won't threaten you but I expect much of you"), of trust (until abused), and of decency (the values of fairness, generosity, and tolerance).

8. The principal and teachers should perceive themselves as generalists first (teachers and scholars in general education) and specialists second (experts in one particular discipline).

9. Ultimate administrative and budget targets should include . . . substantial time for collective planning by teachers, competitive salaries for staff, and an ultimate per pupil cost not to exceed that at traditional schools by more than 10%.

10. The school should demonstrate nondiscriminatory and inclusive policies, practices, and pedagogies. It should model democratic practices that involve all who are directly affected by the school. The school should honor diversity. . . .

For a full version of the Ten Common Principles, go to www.essentialschools.org.

One of the most tangible ways we tend to our community is through our advisory program. Every student in the school is part of an advisory, a group of ten to twelve students who meet together for approximately two and a half hours over the course of each week with an adult, most often one of their teachers. Advisory is one of the central means through which we personalize a student's experience at Parker. The focus is twofold: on building relationships and knowing the whole child well so that the advisor can act as an advocate for the child within the school; and also on creating a supportive and caring peer network that takes into account students' developmental needs and provides a safe environment where students can share feelings, check assumptions, and learn about themselves while still feeling accepted by their peers. Thus, the advisory program affords students the time and space to know one another well and to develop relationships with one another and with their advisor. With these relationships as a backdrop, our advisory program specifically addresses four stated purposes: academic advising, community service, community conversations, and recreation. It is in the context of academic advising that the Personal Learning Plan (PLP) is grounded.

Personal Learning Plans

PLPs have been a part of our students' experience since the school's inception. The document itself is, quite simply, an articulation of a student's strengths, his goals for the school year, and the strategies he will employ to help attain those goals. Equally important as the document itself is the process that leads to its creation and follows with its use. The PLP forms the basis for personalizing students' academic experiences. It creates a process that allows students to articulate their goals for the year, reflect on their progress, and increasingly recognize that they are central in their own learning. The PLP and the process of its creation support the advisor's ability to know the student well so he can effectively advocate for the student and facilitate the student's ability to advocate for herself. It also creates a means by which classroom teachers can tailor curriculum, instruction, and assessment based upon the knowledge of individual students' goals and those goals held in common within a class. Finally, PLPs engage parents and guardians in the dialogue about what matters most to students and how best to support their learning.

The PLP Process

The process of crafting PLPs has evolved over time at Parker, although at its core, it has remained true to the idea of personalizing a student's experience, knowing students well, improving curriculum, instruction, and assessment, and involving parents. In essence, the process has six stages: Beginning the PLP Process and Preparing for the Fall Conference; the Fall Conference itself; Writing the PLP and Creating Access for all Teachers; Using the PLP—Working Toward Goals, Reflecting, and Revising; the Spring Conference; and Year-End Closure.

Beginning the PLP Process and Preparing for the Fall PLP Conference

The PLP process begins at the start of the year in both advisories and academic classes. It is a time of information gathering and thoughtful reflection in anticipation of the Fall PLP Conference, which takes place in the third week of October.

In advisory, students and their advisor begin the year by getting to know one another. Advisors ask questions designed to encourage students to reflect upon their strengths, their learning styles, the things that cause them to feel anxious or excited about the year, and how they feel about their classes thus far. Students are asked to think about their homework level, their level of participation in class, and encouraged to think honestly about their initial sense of the year. They review Parker's habits of learning and self-assess their progress along a continuum. Crossing academic domains, they consider the habits of inquiry, expression, critical thinking, collaboration, organization, attentiveness, involvement, and reflection.

Parker School Habits of Learning

Inquiry
In both school and daily life, you show intellectual curiosity and wonder about the world. You ask thoughtful questions and seek out their answers.

Expression
In both school and daily life, you communicate honestly what you know or want to know and what you believe or feel.

Critical Thinking
In both school and daily life, you analyze, synthesize, and draw conclusions from information. You generate solutions to problems using both creative and rational thought. You keep an open mind and appreciate different points of view.

Collaboration
In both school and daily life, you contribute to the overall effort of a group. You work well with diverse individuals and in a variety of situations, using effective communication skills (consulting, listening, and speaking).

Organization
In both school and daily life, you sift through ideas and data, arranging them wisely and making sense of them. You come to school prepared with what you will need. You set reasonable goals and then plan and manage your time so as to meet them. You persevere in the face of obstacles.

(Continued)

Attentiveness

In both school and daily life, you focus on the task at hand, observing and taking in the information you need to do it well.

Involvement

In both school and daily life, you take the initiative to participate in the process of learning. You contribute your questions, ideas, and actions in group discussions, activities, and projects.

Reflection

In both school and daily life, you review and think about your actions and the work you produce, with the purpose of learning more.

If they are returning students, they look back on their formal progress reports and PLPs from years past. They may work in pairs, small groups, and the large group to think through potential goals for the year. For example, an advisor will ask her advisees to respond to prompts about their classes, domain-based skill areas, habits of learning, and life outside of academics. Advisees will pair up with each other, share their responses to the prompts, ask each other clarifying questions, and listen for patterns; then switch partners and share out again. In the end, they will articulate two to four potential goals for the year that they will bring to the conversation at the conference.

October Pre-PLP Check-in

Name:

Part One: Classes

You have four classes here at Parker. Think about them now. For each class, please comment on the following:

General: How is class going for you? Do you like it? What are you learning?

Workload: What is your workload? How often do you complete your homework? How long does it take you to do it? How do you feel about it?

Effort: What kind of effort are you putting into class? Are you satisfied with it?

Engagement/Participation: How often do you participate? In what ways? What types of activities engage you most?

Other: What else do you need/want to say about this class and your learning in it?

Part Two: Skills

1. Look over the skill areas in all the domains. Pick three you feel are your strengths. Give examples of successes you have had with these skills.

2. Look over the skill areas in all the domains. Pick three that you feel are most troubling/difficult for you. Write about your experiences with them over the last few years. Which might you like to focus on this year? How would you approach them?

Part Three: Habits of Learning

1. Look over the habits of learning. Pick two you feel are your strengths. Why are these strengths? How did you develop these habits?

2. Look over the habits of learning. Pick two that you feel are most troubling/difficult for you. Write about your experiences with them over the last few years. Which might you like to focus on this year? How would you approach them?

Part Four: Outside of Academics

1. Think about the activities you are involved in this year. What do you enjoy about these activities? Which of your strengths help you succeed in them?

2. Think about the activities you might want to try new this year. Which might you like to focus on? How would you approach them?

Part Five: Partnering

1. Pair up with another person in advisory and share your responses to part one. Ask clarifying questions of one another. Reflect on any patterns that you hear.

(Continued)

2. Pair up with a different person and share your responses to part two: clarify and reflect.

3. Pair up with a third person and share your responses to part three: clarify and reflect.

4. Pair up with a fourth person and share your responses to part four: clarify and reflect.

Part Six: Initial Goal Setting

1. Based on the conversations you have just had, write two to four goals for the year.

2. Brainstorm possible strategies you could employ to reach these goals.

Meanwhile in classes, students have taken the first six weeks or so to acclimate to their coursework a bit, are beginning to engage in the first unit of the year, are completing daily work, and are turning in their first formally assessed pieces of the year. Their teachers are continually giving them warm and cool feedback as informal feedback and are asking students to reflect on their progress in domain-specific skills and the habits of learning. Students at Parker study within major intellectual domains: arts and humanities; math, science, and technology; Spanish; and wellness. The domain-specific skills for which we have outlined "Criteria for Excellence" include reading, writing, artistic expression, scientific investigation, mathematical problem-solving, mathematical communication, research, systems thinking, technology, oral presentation, listening, Spanish, and wellness. Student work is assessed in these skill areas via rubrics that assess student progress along a continuum from just beginning, to approaching, to meeting, to exceeding the standard. Each student is expected to meet the school's standards; when this happens consistently, students exhibit their work in public roundtables, or "gateways," thus enabling them to move into the next division of study and ultimately to graduate.

Throughout the fall of each year, teachers ask students to think specifically about goals related to their work in each academic domain. In arts and humanities (AH) class, a teacher might ask students to participate in a four corners exercise around the AH skills and the habits of learning to explore where students feel they have strengths and where they believe they need to improve. In math, science, and technology (MST) class, a teacher might ask students to look back on their most favorite and least favorite project in MST to date, reflect on why those projects still hold meaning for them, and consider what strengths they brought to that work and to think about what challenges it presented. In Spanish, teachers might ask students to go through their existing portfolios and then ask the class to brainstorm as many goals as they can think of related to progress in Spanish. They would then ask students to pick one or two goals that really resonate with them, record them on paper, and reflect on what they will need to do in order to accomplish those goals. In wellness, a teacher might ask students to come up with a personal goal related to their own health and fitness and think about what it will take to meet that goal.

Ultimately, students can look within and across domains for goals that are important to them and that are worth working toward over the course of a year. Whether in advisory or in classes, they are asked to work individually, in pairs, and in small groups to determine what are, in fact, their real hopes for themselves. The message we intentionally send to students is that "you are not alone in this," that we learn best in collaboration, and that we will support each other in reaching our goals.

By the second week in October, the conversations expand beyond advisory and individual classrooms. Teachers have completed the Academic Check-in and advisors have completed the Advisory Check-In, two documents that comment on a student's progress to date and whose purpose is to facilitate communication among and between the teachers who work with each student. The Academic Check-in is a "worksheet" developed by teachers that is used among the team to note the early observations of teachers, as well as to document progress on assessments, homework, class participation, and any other relevant information that may be useful in the conference or the development of the PLP. The Advisory Check-in similarly documents the early activities and endeavors of the advisory group, with particular emphasis on individual students' participation. Early patterns can be identified for discussion through these documents, such as a student's tendency to arrive late to advisory, or a general observation of a student's apparent shyness. The Advisory Check-in provides a potential focus for conversation and creates space for learning goals not directly tied to one academic domain but rather important personal growth to be included in the PLP.

Advisors receive copies of Academic and Advisory Check-ins in advance of the PLP conference, and copies are also mailed home to parents or guardians to be considered in preparation for the PLP conference. Included in the mailing to the parents is a reminder of their child's scheduled PLP conference time and a worksheet for the parents to fill out in preparation for the conference. With prompts similar to the ones students have responded to, parents are asked to discuss their child's strengths, areas in need of improvement, and homework habits. They are also asked about their hopes for their child for the year, hopes that often extend beyond academic achievement and toward personal development. Asking parents to think about these things before the conference ensures that they arrive fully prepared to engage in the conversation.

Time is purposely set aside at this point for "kid talk" among teachers and advisors. In divisional meetings that take place during regularly scheduled faculty meeting time, teachers literally talk about the kids. They share specific anecdotes and student work. They look for patterns that could offer greater insight into how a student is approaching and understanding school and the work she is being asked to do. They share the domain-specific goals that a student has generated in class and suggest possible strategies that will help the student achieve them. And they talk about other factors that might impact that student's success this year, whether those factors relate to an identified learning disability or a situation at home. The advisor (who most often is one of the student's teachers as well) listens, adds his perspective, and takes notes, as he will serve as the "voice" of the teachers during the PLP conference itself.

A Student Perspective: Anne's Story

Even before I was a Parker student, I was a goal-oriented person. I knew what I wanted to achieve and would come up with ideas on how to reach my goals. The process of writing down my goals with my parents and my advisor helped me in two main ways: it reminded me of what I wanted and informed others of that.

Although I come up with goals naturally, I find that when I write them down, they become more real. I felt more obligations to actually complete them. I often walk into PLP conferences saying, "I don't need this. I've already thought out what I need to do!" However, I often walk out with a clearer idea on how to achieve what I want to do. I think this is true for many Parker students. We like to think that we understand what we want and how to do it, but by talking it over with other people, it becomes more real and we more clearly understand how to reach our goals.

One thing I really like about PLP goals is that the goals you set do not have to be purely academic. I am a person who likes to be very busy and so some of my goals have been about balancing school and other activities. This allows me to use my PLP goals to not just improve my schoolwork but also my daily life. I appreciate that Parker acknowledges that people need to make goals about their lives in school and out of school. If I can improve one aspect of my life, then the rest of it (including my schoolwork and my attitude about school) will change.

When my advisor knows my goals, she can encourage me to work to achieve them. One year, I was co-directing a play while I was "gateway-ing" from one division to the next and was worried that I would get over-whelmed with work. When I told my advisor about this at my PLP meeting, she helped me come up with a way to make my project a part of that play. She also would ask me how both the project and the play were going from time to time, so that if I got into a stressful situation, I had the oppor-tunity to talk to her about it and get help with it. I really felt supported by my teacher in reaching both my goals of directing a play and midyear gate-waying, and I liked that she did not encourage me to concentrate only on my academic goal but helped me find a way to achieve both of them with-out compromising my stress level.

Although PLP day means to some students a day off, it means to oth-ers a day to understand their goals. Students who take advantage of PLP goals are able to understand what they need to do and to have their parents and teachers understand what they are working towards. This is important because if a student is not only aware of what they want to achieve but also supported by others to achieve it, they will be more successful.

Anne Dufault graduated in 2008. She was a co-leader of the school's Justice Committee. Her outside interests include theater, singing, and directing.

The Fall Conference

By the third week in October, all three "voices" vital to the creation of the PLP are ready to be heard, and it is during the Fall PLP Conference that that dialogue takes place. Instead of regular classes, the student, her parents or guardians, and advisor meet for thirty to forty-five minutes to discuss the year so far and to come to consensus around that student's goals for the year and the strategies needed to achieve them. The conference itself is quite structured, using a specific PLP conference protocol in order to ensure that every voice is heard and that the conversation stays focused on the development of the PLP. Any concerns that come up in the conference outside of goal creation are noted by the advisor and addressed at another time.

Conference Protocol

Two minutes—Welcome by advisor who states goal of the conference and reviews agenda.

Five minutes—Student shares his or her experience, strengths, and needs based on prep work he or she has done.

Five minutes—Parent shares his or her observations of the child and his or her hopes for the child based on prep work he or she has done.

Five minutes—Advisor shares his or her observations of the student's strengths and needs, as well as those documented by the student's teacher in the progress reports.

Ten minutes—Advisor, student, and parent reflect on any patterns that have emerged around strengths, needs, habits of learning, and skill development. From those patterns, identify three to four goals for the year and possible strategies for reaching them.

Three minutes—Advisor brings conference to closure by explaining the next steps in the PLP process (writing or revising the PLP, follow-up through the year) and by asking for any feedback on the conference itself.

The conference begins with an introduction by the advisor and a review of the conference protocol. The student is asked to speak first (with her preparatory documents in hand), summarizing the work she has done in advance of the conference in advisory and in classes, and expressing the goals she hopes to work toward in the coming year. Next, her parents or guardians are asked to share their observations and hopes, often speaking from the prompts that were sent home. And finally, the advisor speaks on behalf of himself and the student's teachers, articulating strengths and perceived needs. Once everyone has had a chance to speak, the dialogue around emerging patterns of strengths, needs, and possible goals takes place. The advisor takes notes throughout this conversation in order to capture the best of everyone's thinking and to shed light on where consensus is forming. Occasionally, the advisor may reflect back to the student and parents what he has heard as a way of maintaining accuracy and tending to the sometimes nuanced articulations that sometimes occur when students or parents are speaking from the heart. As the consensus around goals emerges, the advisor shifts the conversation toward a brainstorming of strategies that the student can use to reach those goals. At the end of the conference, it is the advisor's job to review all that has been discussed and to highlight the goals upon which everyone has agreed. Typically, three to four goals will be generated, some with specific strategies fully fleshed out, others not. Advisors will explain that over the next two weeks, advisors and, in the case of our oldest students, students will be writing the actual PLP document. They will be finding the right wording and adding details as needed. Upon completion, the PLP will be mailed home to the parents or guardians, who will have a chance to offer feedback as well, though in our experience few revisions are made after that point. It is important to note that thoughtful preparation, careful listening, and honest communication create the conditions for the articulation of a document that accurately expresses all participants' hopes for the year.

Writing the PLP and Creating Access for All Teachers

To support advisors and older students as they write the PLP, we have documented dozens of common PLP goals and strategies as a reference guide. We have also created computerized templates that provide a basic outline for the PLP (and makes the organization and distribution of PLPs infinitely easier). In some years, we have also dedicated faculty meeting time to the writing of PLPs.

Several things need to be kept in mind when writing the PLP. First, the summary of the student's strengths should include academic as well as personal strengths. Second, the goals should be attainable within a year and measurable in some way so that progress toward them can be documented. Third, the goals and strategies should be written in terms of what the student will do rather than what the teacher or advisor will do. And fourth, the goals are best when they take root in the student's own best hopes for the coming year. For example, Debbie's goal might be that she will improve her reading skills over the course of the year. As Debbie works toward improving her reading skills, three strategies she might employ include the following: Debbie will respond to what she is reading by answering specific prompts in her reading journal; Debbie will mark important passages with comments in the margin and will summarize those passages in her own words after reading; Debbie will read a book of her own choosing for pleasure.

PLP goals themselves can focus on a range of things: specific domain-based skills, completion of the work necessary to "gateway" from one division to the next, a specific habit of learning, a means of personal growth, or an attempt at something new. The PLPs of our seniors are different from those of younger students and reflect the transition to independence and autonomy they will soon be making. The Senior PLP includes a section on the Graduation Portfolio, the Senior Project, and Life After Parker.

Sample PLP Goals and Strategies

Goal: Student will be an active participant in class.

Strategies:

1. On a weekly basis, student will keep track of the times he voluntarily spoke in class. On a piece of paper, the student will write a mark every time he participates or attempts to participate. Each week, he should try to participate at least one more time than in the previous week.

2. Student will write at least one question in regard to homework to ask in class the next day.

3. Student will make an effort to share his ideas, questions, reactions, and even partially formed thoughts in class discussions on a regular basis. Student will "share it!" when he has an idea to contribute. Student will also write first, during, or before conversation to organize and articulate his ideas before sharing.

4. Student will ask questions when he is confused by something.

Goal: Student will manage his time responsibly.

Strategies:

1. Student will use her assignment book for every class, every day. Student will create a calendar of due dates.

2. Student will create a pro/con list when she needs to make a decision or balance an academic and an extracurricular activity with the time she has.

3. Student will set aside a specific homework time each evening. Before beginning, student will come up with a few goals to accomplish and plan for how much time she should realistically spend on each homework goal. Student will strive to "know when to say when" by spending focused scheduled periods of time on specific tasks and stopping when the designated time is up.

4. Student will participate in advisory activities about using time well and making schedules.

Goal: Student will improve mathematical comprehension and confidence.

Strategies:

1. Student will attend after school MST once a week.

2. Student will break down large problems into simpler problems and document that work.

3. Student will read instructions, start problem, and then reread instructions.

4. Student will write down specific questions she has and ask them.

The act of writing the PLP is an important one. The formal documentation of what is essentially an intimate conversation, though potentially daunting, provides a sense of grounding and commitment for students. Seeing her own hopes and goals recorded on paper "sets" those commitments and makes explicit the direction for the school year and attests to our mutual commitment to supporting the student as she works hard on her own behalf.

Once all PLPs are written and turned in, the process of disseminating them begins. We are aided in this process by the use of a computer program that can sort PLPs as needed. Each advisor receives a copy of the PLP for each of her advisees and places it in the advisee's advisory folder for later use. Teachers receive the PLPs for all of the students they teach and keep them close at hand for meetings with their domain, division, or teaching partner. At one time, this was an overwhelming copying and sorting job that was imperfect at best. We are relieved that it is now much more manageable. It has been critical for us as a school staff to think pragmatically about the systems we had, and more pointedly, about the ones we needed to create in order to become efficient in disseminating and distributing the PLPs. No matter how useful and articulate the PLPs were or their potential for helping our students, without careful refinement of the very practical elements of reproducing and distributing the documents, we could not uphold our responsibilities to supporting students' learning informed by their Personal Learning Plans.

Using the PLP: Working Toward Goals, Reflecting, Revising

Once PLPs have been distributed, it is time to take a deep breath. It takes a lot of energy to prepare for, create, write, and disseminate the PLP, and everyone involved deserves a little reprieve and a pat on the back. But soon after this pause, PLP work begins anew in advisories and in classes. Typically, advisors check in individually with advisees each week to make sure they are implementing the strategies articulated in their PLPs. These check-ins take place during morning connections and afternoon reflections and might be considered more informal in nature. For example, "Debbie, you are staying today for afterschool help with your MST teacher, right?" "Teri, can I see your planner to make sure you've got your homework written down for tonight?" Every four to six weeks for the remainder of the school year, advisors ask advisees to undertake a more formal reflection on their progress toward their goals. This may include responding to specific prompts, noting progress in one's PLP log book, or using the PLP peer reflection protocol. The PLP peer reflection protocol is a particularly powerful tool, as advisees are asked to listen to one another, provide support, offer suggestions, and, in a way, be accountable to someone other than their advisor.

PLP Peer Reflection Protocol

Take a minute and look over your PLP to review your goals and your strategies.

Take notes on your PLP—what is working, what is not?

In groups of three, number yourselves 1–3.

1. Person 1 talks about his or her first goal for 2 minutes, including questions he or she may have, the reason for the goal, etc.

2. Persons 2 and 3—offer suggestions, strategies, similar situations, ideas for helping. Person 2 asks the following questions and person 3 **takes notes**.

3. After one person has gone through all his or her goals, switch roles until you are finished.

Name of person reflecting on goals:

Goal #1:

Why is this goal important to you?

What specific steps have you taken to work on this goal **already**?

Have you made progress on this goal? How do you know (**specifics here**)?

What are your next steps to work on this goal?

How can I help you in the next month in working on this goal?

Goal #2:

Why is this goal important to you?

What specific steps have you taken to work on this goal **already**?

Have you made progress on this goal? How do you know (**specifics here**)?

(Continued)

What are your next steps to work on this goal?

How can I help you in the next month in working on this goal?

Goal #3:

Why is this goal important to you?

What specific steps have you taken to work on this goal **already**?

Have you made progress on this goal? How do you know (**specifics here**)?

What are your next steps to work on this goal?

How can I help you in the next month in working on this goal?

The release of progress reports, our formal academic reporting mechanism, also provides opportunities for students to reflect on their progress in relation to their teachers' perceptions of their development.

At the same time students are working with their PLPs in advisory, teachers dedicate time in their domain, divisional or teaching partner meetings, or both, to looking at the PLPs of the students they teach. They look at what individual students are working toward and are able to speak directly to those goals when writing students' assessments and progress reports. They also chart the different types of goals students have in common among their classes. In doing so, they are able to look for patterns that can then inform their choices in curriculum, instruction, and assessment.

If collaboration is a common goal, the teacher may decide to replace an independent learning activity with one that requires that students work cooperatively. If a critical number of students need to improve research skills, the teacher might rethink a unit of study to provide additional opportunities for students to practice their research skills. If many students in a class intend to "gateway," then the teacher may build in additional time for revision. If several students are hoping to increase their comfort in conversational Spanish, the teacher may create more opportunities for speaking.

There are times when a student attains a PLP goal at the midyear, for example, trying out for and participating in the school play or midyear "gatewaying" from one division to the next. That success is documented in the student's advisory folder on her PLP and, sometimes, a student will create a new goal in its place. Other times, she will refocus her energy to her other PLP goals.

While the primary focus of PLPs is on students and their achievement in school, a natural byproduct of the PLP is in its serving as an entry point for conversation among students and parents and advisor. The PLP allows parents a legitimate place in initiating or participating in conversations about school with their student or their child's advisor. The PLP serves as a tacit invitation to parents to be and remain connected to their child's progress.

The Spring Conference

In early March, we formally reconvene for the Spring PLP Conference. In our Division 1 advisories, this conference serves as a formal check-in for advisor, student, and parents or guardians alike on progress made toward the PLP goals. Again, there is a protocol that ensures each person has a voice. Success is applauded, revisions are made, particularly on strategies that aren't working, and renewed emphasis is placed on goals as needed. In Division 2, the emphasis shifts somewhat to specific student work and to their portfolios, as the transition into Division 2 can be challenging for many students. In our senior advisories, the focus of the conference is on readiness for graduation, the senior project, and life after Parker.

Year-End Closure

Reflection upon progress made continues throughout the remainder of the school year and is documented in advisory folders. As students and advisor look back over the year together, they are often surprised by how well they have gotten to know each other and how well they were able to move through those moments that were most difficult. Advisors ask their advisees to write year-end reflections and celebrate everyone's success whether one goal or all have been achieved. For some students, this can be a particularly challenging request because it asks them to stay in a reflective mode at the end of the year when, most often, students just want to move on. For some, it can be just as hard to look at their successes and to celebrate them as it is for others to confront their areas of weakness. It is this final synthesis of the year that becomes the groundwork for the following school year. Some students will move on to a new advisor and carry with them the artifacts of this advisory experience. Others will continue with the same advisor, particularly in Division 1. We have learned that the relationships developed among and between students, advisors, and parents helps provide a solid foundation for success in school. For many students, a sense of continuity allows for a smoother transition the following September.

Challenges

Our PLP process is not without pitfalls, and we have addressed our share of problems over the years. When faced with one of these challenges, we very deliberately carve out time as a full faculty, in divisional and domain meetings, and in conversations with students and parents to reflect on what is and isn't working and to revise the process as needed. For example, when the PLP started to become a paper filed away in a drawer and only pulled out every few months, we asked ourselves how the PLP might be a more living, useful, and central force in our students' learning and created a mechanism for using PLPs more intentionally on a daily basis. When folks became overwhelmed by the layers of paperwork and the system of distributing PLPs, we streamlined and computerized the process in order to provide better access for and to facilitate better communication among advisors, teachers, students, and parents. When new advisors felt they needed more guidance, we looked at the ways we could build additional training into the process. When older students expressed that the relevance/usefulness of the PLP changed as they progressed through the divisions, we created a new PLP document for seniors that better reflects what is of importance to them at this time in their lives. When Division 2 advisors felt the emphasis of the spring conference should be different for their students, we collectively crafted a different conference protocol.

What we have learned from all of these challenges is the importance of continually reflecting upon the PLP process: whether that means providing more or less or different support at each stage; reviewing the documents that detail the PLP process to see whether, in practice, they truly reflect our intentions; revising the ways we prepare students, parents, and advisors; or facilitating better communication so as to make the PLP more central to student learning.

By creating an environment where questions are continually invited and raised and by giving everyone involved in the process an opportunity to revise and rethink the PLP process, we gain the trust and support of our community.

Professional Development and Support for Advisors

We deliberately utilize considerable professional development time to support advisors. Parker's advisory coordinator actively leads teachers through the

PLP process and facilitates faculty meeting time that focuses on every aspect of the PLP. For example, the advisory coordinator may ask the faculty to participate in role plays of PLP conferences and to look for common threads that reveal the elements of successful conferences. The advisory coordinator provides advisors with tools they can use to help their students become more reflective of the progress they have made toward their PLP goals. Virtually everything is documented from time lines to preparation guides to sample parent letters to PLP protocols to reflection activities so that no one faculty member feels alone in this work.

We not only ask students to set goals and monitor and reflect on their progress toward those goals, we expect teachers at Parker to do the same. A structured component of our professional development program requires teachers to set goals of their own choosing, create a plan to reach those goals in consultation with their domain leader, reflect upon and document their progress, and share what they have learned with their colleagues in Critical Friends Groups, domain meetings, and other settings.

Lessons Learned

At the end of the day what we hope most for is for students to become reflective learners and take responsibility for their own learning. We want advisors to know their students well so that they can advocate for the whole child and help their advisees grow into an effective advocate for themselves. We want teachers to pay careful attention to the students they are teaching and to make decisions about curriculum, instruction, and assessment to best meet those students' needs. We want parents to feel welcome in the school, to fully engage in discussions about their child's learning, and to trust that goals and priorities make sense for their child.

We have to come realize that at Parker, becoming a skilled teacher is inextricably linked with becoming a skilled advisor. We have also learned that the processes and structures we put in place must explicitly reflect our core beliefs and values about teaching and learning. We cherish equally our teachers' dedication to the study of intellectual disciplines and their commitment to the development of young people. Although it may seem daunting to teachers to imagine carrying these expectations, our experience at Parker suggests to us that it is only when we know our students well that we are able to expect so much from them. It is only when students come to know themselves well with the support of their parents and teachers that they come to realize that there are no limits to what they can accomplish.

Reflection Questions

1. What's missing at your school that personal learning plans could address?

2. Do you know your students' histories, hopes, dreams, fears, and goals? How can you learn these things about your students?

3. How can you use these things to improve student performance?

4. If your school is already using student portfolios, how can you push the envelope to allow for students to use them for exhibitions, college preparation, and exploring life choices?

5. How will or does your school assess student portfolios?

Resources

The Big Picture Company, www.bigpicture.org

Clarke, J. (2003). *Changing Systems to Personalize Learning: Personalized Learning.* Providence, RI: Northeast and Islands Regional Educational Laboratory. Download at http://www.alliance.brown.edu/db/ea_catalog.php

Clarke, J., & DiMartino, J. (1999) *Personal Plans for Progress: Forming the Basis for High School Reform.* Providence, RI: Northeast and Islands Regional Educational Laboratory.

DiMartino, J., & Clarke, J. (2008). *Personalizing the High School Experience for Each Student.* Alexandria, VA: ASCD.

DiMartino, J., Clarke, J., & Wolk, D. (eds.) (2003). *Personalized Learning: Preparing High School Students to Create Their Futures.* Lanham, MD: Rowman & Littlefield.

PART TWO

Making Learning Personal

Curriculum

*Changing Instructional Practice and the
Long Path to Project-Based Learning*

Paul Curtis

New Technology High School, Napa, California

In the mid 1990s, the small San Francisco suburban town of Napa, California, did something significant. They chose to create a new kind of high school designed for the twenty-first century. At the time, the business community was seeking to revitalize and diversify its economic base by attracting high tech companies and high-paying jobs to complement the tourism and wine industries already established in the valley. These business leaders were among the first to realize that the key to creating a twenty-first century economy was to create a prepared workforce.

The school board and community leaders knew that unlike previous generations, Napa's young people would be unlikely to earn a living wage with only a high school diploma. Schools that focused solely on state academic standards and minimum graduation requirements were not going to create a well-rounded student suitable for either the college environment or the office. Students needed skills like creative thinking, problem solving, collaboration, and technology use to be ready for postsecondary education, and high-skilled work to be competitive in the workplace.

The two existing 2,500 student high schools in Napa were "good schools" by most state and community standards. They had academic programs that helped prepare students for applying to college, but did little to prepare them for the independent learning required to be successful once accepted. Even more alarming, Napa's traditional high schools were not configured to equip all students with the skills needed to achieve high-paying jobs in a technology-rich, global economy.

The Napa Unified School District's school board, working with the business community, decided that rather than trying to change the comprehensive high schools, they would create a model school that would incubate innovative ideas and become a learning opportunity for the rest of the district's staff. Nearly four years of planning went into the new school as they conducted site visits, held focus groups, and researched best practices. In 1996, the doors were opened to a new high school in Napa that, except for its students, didn't look anything like a high school. It had glass walls, an office-like environment, computer-filled classrooms, and there were no lockers or hall monitors. Students worked in groups on projects, presented in front of each other and community members, and took college classes. It wasn't long before New Technology High school was getting attention as a school to see.

Since its creation, New Tech High has seen more than three thousand visiting educators wandering its halls on student-led tours. These visitors continue to come to learn how the school works and which parts they can take back to their own schools. They come with lots of questions about the school's technology, about its test scores and, of course, about its instructional methodology. It is in this quest for tidbits of change that the folly of many education reform efforts is exposed.

New Tech High didn't evolve its way to become a twenty-first century school. New Tech did not adopt pilot programs or attempt partial implementation of new teaching methods. New Tech was created to be a twenty-first century school from the ground up. Although the facilities were originally designed to be an elementary school, every process and paradigm, including the architecture and paint scheme, was rethought and reorganized around the school's purpose. This can't be said for other attempts at reform.

The Plague of Piecemeal Reform

On my last day of teaching in a traditional, suburban, comprehensive high school, my friends and colleagues honored me with the Don Quixote award. It was a construction hard hat that they had painted gold with a note referencing my various attempts to "tilt at the windmills" of education reform during my seven years there. I didn't realize it then, but my experiences in the traditional school did as much to shape my perspectives of school reform as almost anything else. So I thought it might be wise to start the story here.

At our core, I think most teachers are idealists who strive to help every child succeed. It would be hard to explain the time and personal money teachers spend on their students if it were not so. Most teachers start out pretty optimistic about their ability to create the kind of classroom that they think is best for students. When new ideas come up that show promise in making schools better for students, most are willing to give them a shot. When government officials, superintendents, principals, and teachers hear about a successful new program or approach, they attempt to bring it back to their school districts and lay it over the existing systems and structures already in place. Unfortunately, these systems and structures are often at odds with the new program, and they begin to push back against the change that is disrupting the system. Without significant extra energy or money, the system is quick to restore the old order at the expense of the new ideas. Two examples from my own experience can help illustrate the problem.

The first occurred when my traditional comprehensive school considered moving to longer blocks that met every other day for 110 minutes instead of the typical daily 55-minute period. As expected, staff members argued the merits of both schedule types, so the principal took a group of teachers to a school a few counties over that had supposedly made this transition successfully. Several of us packed ourselves onto school busses for the drive and, upon our arrival, were given a quick introduction and let loose on the campus with a map and bell schedule for classroom observations. As a social studies teacher, I headed to an economics course with the hopes of finding something really fantastic. Instead, I watched a teacher lecture for two hours straight. It was obvious the teacher was very accustomed to being on center stage and had taken his two days' worth of lectures and lined them up back to back for the long block. The students were polite but unengaged as I sat in the back of the class listening to his monologue. I was reminded of the scene from *Ferris Bueller's Day Off*, "Anyone . . . Anyone." I could imagine that same teacher in the staff room complaining that block schedules can't work because kids can't pay attention that long. He's right, but I don't think very many adults could either.

The problem was not with the schedule, it was that the instructional practices were not in line with the schedule. Teachers come to define "learning" by their own experiences in high school, college, and credentialing programs. Unfortunately, very few teachers were exposed to 110 minute blocks, project-based learning, or authentic assessment practices in their own education.

It takes much more than a two-day workshop to prepare teachers to change this entrenched definition and make the best use of the extra time provided by block scheduling. The school we visited had clearly failed to properly train its staff to use more student-centered approaches to instruction to take advantage of the longer blocks.

Instead of taking on the challenge of tackling the block schedule, sufficiently training the teachers in new instructional practices, and negotiating a more authentic teacher evaluation system, school leaders were conservative and hoped that by changing one thing, it would lead to changes in other areas. By tackling only the schedule, it became the wrench in the gears of an otherwise smoothly running machine, and the system worked to remove it. The same outcome would be expected had the school spent two weeks training teachers to implement project-based learning and then left the schedule in 55-minute blocks. More often than not, this piecemeal approach leads to failure after failure of reform initiatives as the institutional systems reassert the original order and unintentionally create a group of cynical teachers ready to resist the next effort.

My second example comes from the mid-1990s when my school district was awarded a U.S. Department of Education Carl Perkins grant for creating small learning communities around career paths (SLCs). Working with teachers, the district created several academies around various themes, including telecommunications, health and human services, international studies, and business. Each small learning community had a team of teachers that shared a group of students allowing for curriculum integration and more personalized learning. As a member of the business-themed academy, I was teamed up with English, math, and science teachers, as well as three vocational education teachers representing manufacturing and administration. At the end of the first year, the school board asked our students to present how the new small learning communities were working. Our students reported on significant grade increases, their sense of community compared to the anonymity of the larger campus, and actually wanting to come to school.

These student improvements were not lost on the school's counseling office. Because the academy staff didn't control student recruitment to the program, the school counselors enrolled a large number of at-risk students into our program the following year. They were well intentioned, thinking that the smaller learning community would help these students attain success, and in fact, it did. Unfortunately, the academy quickly grew a reputation among the parents and students as the "dummy academy," which resulted in an exodus of our average and talented students. That year, our common planning time was spent focused on disciplinary issues instead of curriculum development. The following year, because we didn't control our staffing or schedule, we lost our English teacher and our common planning period. Despite our successes, the larger school was not organized in a way to support the SLCs and began to whittle away at the elements that had made it successful. It's not hard to predict what happened next. Among the half-dozen programs started with the grant money, all were dismantled within five years. Some were reduced to single elective options, others were gone without a trace.

It is much clearer to me now why those career academies failed to take hold despite early successes and a motivated teaching staff. Like the block scheduling example, trying to make piecemeal changes without altering the fundamental support systems dooms the effort to failure. Organizations put systems in place to help make them more efficient. These systems resist change, and unless made to the entire structure, meaningful change is nearly impossible to sustain. Schools wishing to change the instructional practices in the classroom need to change the cultures, policies, and practices that support them—all of them, all at once. It's easy to say you want teachers to implement project-based learning; it is much harder to change the systems that, left untouched, will push teachers back to traditional approaches.

A Student Perspective: Lauren's Story

On my first day, I knew immediately that New Technology High School was different—computers on every table, glass walls, and classroom seating focused on interaction among students as opposed to in rows looking at the teacher. Throughout my time there, I developed the technological savvy that defines the "Tech" of New Tech. I learned how to use word processing, spreadsheet, and presentation tools. I designed a website, and I used multimedia and imaging programs. More important, I learned that one of New Tech's greatest successes comes from placing the student in the "driver's seat" through project-based learning.

(Continued)

Before transferring to New Tech, I attended a college-preparatory high school for my freshman and sophomore years. I was an A student, yet became apathetic regarding the learning process and certainly uninspired to continue on to higher education. I would sit in class thinking, "How am I supposed to get excited about the world by copying notes from an overhead projector, then taking an exam on it?" My parents recognized this in me and suggested that I check out New Technology High School.

My first year at New Tech included an integrated history and English course called American Studies. My classmates and I were given an assignment to create an informative website describing a movement in American history during a designated time period. A fellow student and I decided to document the development of union laws. Our understanding was developed through the use of traditional classroom resources and those on the Internet. We used documents, articles, witness accounts, and photographs to determine the cause and effects of the labor movement. As a result of our growing personal passion for the subject, our research led us to an investigation on current global working conditions. I had never felt such emotion in a school project as I did during our research on sweatshops. We went beyond our assigned project and created a site tracing popular fashion items to the pitiful labor conditions and wages that produced them. When as a student you are directing your own education, there is a feeling of discovery and enthusiasm that reaches beyond the subject at hand.

I've found that I consistently rely upon the skills and abilities developed at New Tech. My biggest fear was that I might be unprepared for the traditional academic work of college. During my freshman year at MIT, I participated in a course that investigated the complex problem of monitoring and preserving the Amazon rain forest. This was a very open-ended project in which the students were required to determine the structure. Many of my classmates had never encountered such a task—their previous experience primarily involved bookwork and exams. Some of them had never worked in groups, delivered presentations, or defended the results of their own findings. Although I had very little technical background on the subject, I fell very naturally into the dynamics of this project due to my experience at New Tech. I was confidently able to adapt and be a leader in the situation and to figure out the steps necessary to achieve our final product. I believe that my curiosity and passion for learning was cultivated at New Tech, and the skills that I developed—critical thinking, self-discipline and time management, communication, and team working—have proven invaluable in nearly every aspect of my life.

Lauren Cooney graduated from New Technology High School in 2002 (its fifth graduating class) as the valedictorian. She then attended Massachusetts Institute of Technology where she received a Bachelor of Science in Mechanical and Ocean Engineering and is currently working toward a Master of Science in Ocean Engineering. As the recipient of a Department of Defense National Defense Science and Engineering Graduate (NDSEG) Fellowship, Lauren is conducting research related to control systems of underwater vehicles.

Hierarchy of Needs for School Change

In the 1950s, Abraham Maslow proposed that humans have a hierarchy of needs. At the bottom of the hierarchy are physical needs (i.e., air, food) and until these needs are met, not much else will take place. At the top of the hierarchy are things like morality and intellectual pursuits. The premise is fairly simple; as much as I want you to focus on the sarcastic wit of William Shakespeare, you would be incapable of doing so if you were choking on a chicken bone. Needs at the bottom of the hierarchy will overshadow items at the top of the hierarchy.

I believe that schools have a very similar hierarchy of needs (see Figure 3.1). At the top of this hierarchy is student success—something every school strives for. At the bottom is school culture, ideally demonstrated by positive, healthy relationships among the staff and students. Again, the premise is pretty simple. As much as I want students in my classroom to be successful, I will be unable to achieve it if the culture of the school is handicapped by poor relationships, threats of violence, or low expectations. Schools cannot expect to see changes in the upper levels of the hierarchy until more basic needs are met.

Because all schools want all students to be academically successful and it is pretty evident that what happens in the classroom (curriculum and instruction) plays an important part in determining student success, it is here that schools will target their efforts. Schools will purchase textbooks with new approaches, adopt managed curriculum, create pacing guides, or train their teachers on authentic assessment in an attempt to improve the instruction. Unfortunately, conditions in the lower levels of the hierarchy such as student absences or too many course preparations will consume the teacher before he can focus on the new idea or program. Without a holistic approach that addresses each level of the hierarchy in ways specifically designed to support the kind of school you want to build, successful change is much less likely to occur.

Too often, education reform efforts fail to see long lasting results due to the plague of piecemeal programs. As an endeavor to "reform," many schools implement new programs and spend millions of dollars without adequate training, staffing and schedule changes, or the autonomies necessary for success. Failing

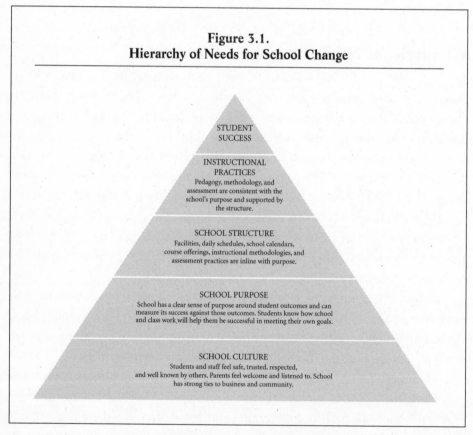

Figure 3.1.
Hierarchy of Needs for School Change

STUDENT
SUCCESS

INSTRUCTIONAL
PRACTICES
Pedagogy, methodology, and
assessment are consistent with the
school's purpose and supported by
the structure.

SCHOOL STRUCTURE
Facilities, daily schedules, school calendars,
course offerings, instructional methodologies, and
assessment practices are inline with purpose.

SCHOOL PURPOSE
School has a clear sense of purpose around student outcomes and can
measure its success against those outcomes. Students know how school
and class work will help them be successful in meeting their own goals.

SCHOOL CULTURE
Students and staff feel safe, trusted, respected,
and well known by others. Parents feel welcome and listened to. School
has strong ties to business and community.

The hierarchy of needs for school change informs us that without addressing issues of culture, purpose, and structure, our attempts to improve instructional practice are very difficult to sustain.

schools become bogged down in test preparation to get test score improvement in the short term without regard for broader learning objectives in the long term. The challenge for educators is to understand the entirety of a school's systems in order to make more fundamental changes at the lower levels of the hierarchy so that the instructional changes are supported and successful.

A Blank Slate

One of the key factors to New Tech High's early success was that it wasn't laid on top of an existing school or program. It had to continue to live within the parameters of the school district, teachers unions, state tests, and budgetary concerns, but New Tech High was allowed to redefine the practices and principles of how a school works. Unlike most schools that attempt reform, New Tech High disassembled the educational and cultural cogs of the traditional school so that a new machine could be created. Because it was a new school, the staff at New Tech High was able to institutionalize reform, making it the norm instead of the exception. Before the doors opened, the creators evaluated current education research, visited successful schools, and studied effective programs. All of that knowledge was integrated into a cohesive plan for redefining every level of the hierarchy to meet the needs of a twenty-first century school.

Culture: Trust, Respect, and Responsibility

In *High Schools on a Human Scale*, Thomas Tock describes the cultural changes experienced when schools become small and personalized. Large schools are challenged to keep students from being anonymous on campus. As a member of a 10-person social studies department in a large traditional school, I ate lunch with my fellow social studies teachers and enjoyed great conversations about curriculum. We never talked about students because none of us shared students. Those teachers were across campus having lunch with their own English, science, or math colleagues. When I came to work at New Tech High with about 100 students per grade level and only eight teachers, individual student progress and success became regular lunchtime topics.

To avoid anonymity in large schools, students join sports teams, band, drama, clubs, or informal cliques that become part of their identity (remember the movie *The Breakfast Club?*). In at-risk school environments, students might choose to join a gang with the hopes of avoiding becoming a victim of the violence that surrounds them. In the smaller school setting of New Tech, it is very easy for students to get past the cliques and stereotypes as they get to know their peers as individuals. Further, because most of our curriculum is project-based, students are constantly working with others and learning the assets that having different types of people can bring to a group.

By keeping the number of students under 400, New Tech High staff can give more personalized attention to students and abandon many of the crowd control mechanisms used at bigger schools. For example, we do not have bells that call students to class. Many visiting teachers are amazed to see that students find their way to class without the traditional Pavlovian response to the tardy bell. This simple change promotes student responsibility and is more in line with the workplace. Of course, we still have students who are tardy, and we respond as an employer might with a personal conversation.

We've also banished another mainstay in big schools: the hall pass. When the adults on campus know nearly every young person by name, the hall pass is no longer needed. The lack of anonymity also curbs theft, truancy, and vandalism. By solving the cultural problems that can exist on large, traditional school campuses, the New Tech staff is free to move up the hierarchy to work on purpose, structure, and instruction.

Purpose: A Focus on Twenty-First Century Skills

In 1990, the U.S. Secretary of Labor commissioned a report that investigated the skills that the nation's young people would need to be successful in the world of work. The result was the Secretary's Commission on Achieving Necessary Skills (S.C.A.N.S.) report, which concluded that basic reading, writing, and math skills were being addressed by the school system. However, there were a host of other skills key to the workplace largely ignored by the traditional curriculum, including collaboration, problem solving, and use of technology. Ten years later, the Partnership for 21st Century Skills reiterated what the S.C.A.N.S. report told us—that the current high school design is not preparing kids for the world of work. If the New Tech approach was going to successfully prepare students for the twenty-first century, it needed to fully incorporate these skills into the curriculum.

New Tech High prioritized workplace skills from the beginning and formalized a set of schoolwide learning outcomes that put those skills into our curriculum.

We used the S.C.A.N.S. report as our base and ended up with a list of eight learning goals for all students: technology literacy, written communication, oral communication, collaboration, critical thinking and problem solving, citizenship and ethics, career preparation, and core content literacy, as shown in Figure 3.2. Notice that we did not separate the twenty-first century skills from the state standards; we included both on the same list. Every teacher at New Tech is expected to work toward student mastery in all of these learning goals. Even our math teachers assign written work and provide an evaluation of spelling, grammar, and mechanics as part of the student's assessment of written communication.

Working with WestEd, an education research group, we developed a student portfolio requirement for all seniors. Graduating students are expected to present evidence of proficiency in each of the learning outcome skill areas via a digital website that they produce. Gradually, the New Tech High's Digital Portfolio has grown into a four-year process of reflection and presentation of each student's skills and abilities.

Like the adoption of the learning outcomes, the portfolio requirement for our students created a structural change for the staff as well. We needed a way to measure, capture, and present student performance in skills that most schools don't bother recording. For example, we sought to provide students with meaningful feedback on their collaboration skills as they worked with their peers on

Figure 3.2.
Twenty-First Century Outcomes

CRITICAL THINKING
COLLABORATION
ORAL COMMUNICATION
WRITTEN COMMUNICATION
TECHNOLOGY LITERACY
CITIZENSHIP AND ETHICS
CAREER PREPARATION
CORE CONTENT LITERACY

projects. I am sure you are familiar with the typical school group project experience in which some students contribute little, others go above and beyond, yet all end up receiving the same grade. We needed a way to capture that performance data and provide fair, consistent feedback to students for improvement.

Our solution was an evaluation rubric that articulated our expectations to students and defined an effective collaborator's behavior. By placing the rubric on the Web and asking students to evaluate their teammates at the end of each project, we captured and reported on student collaboration skills with almost no teacher effort. Students can then view a summary report of peers' scores and comments. This real-time feedback on a critical twenty-first century skill can be used by the student to demonstrate collaboration proficiency in their digital portfolio and is also recorded as part of the student's course grade. In education, what you assess is what you get. Formal feedback around twenty-first century skills makes them important to students and teachers.

The student portfolio requirement also required New Tech teachers to reflect on their own practices. It was not possible for a student to present evidence of great oral presentation skills if they spent their days doing worksheets and answering questions at the end of each textbook chapter. By clearly identifying our school's purpose and evaluation systems around preparing students for the twenty-first century, teachers were pushed to incorporate them into the curriculum.

Structure: New Courses, New Classrooms, New Schedules

Ask people what a classroom of the future looks like and you will probably hear something about computers in nearly every answer. New Tech put enough computers in each classroom for every student and built a robust network to support them. The impact this had on instruction was dramatic. Technology, combined with the other changes, proved to be a powerful lever for change. Teachers once had a monopoly on the information the students saw; the written word of the textbook could be counted on for the "right" answer. In a technology-rich classroom, the Internet is the wild, wild west of information. Students need to be taught to understand the logic of search engines, read with a critical eye, and evaluate the sources of information in every class, every day.

With the Internet, the answers to the most obscure factual questions are now just a few clicks away and can be found with little or no effort. In order to challenge students, teachers are forced to ask much more complicated questions that don't necessarily have a correct answer that can be found on the Web. Asking students to turn in an assignment on the root causes of the Civil War results in students copying and pasting the answers from one of dozens of pages on the Web with that information. Asking students to present and defend a plan to avoid the Civil War and still bring an end to slavery requires the contextual understanding of the causes of the war. Further, there will be no single correct solution (although still an infinite number of incorrect ones) and the test will be to defend their solutions against critics. The computer, the textbook, and even the teacher now become one of many resources the students will use to answer this question. Technology and the Internet, supported by other structural changes, will by their very nature force a change in instructional practice.

Ironically, New Tech High has adopted very little educational software. They instead load the computers with a pretty standard set of business software. Like office workers, the students each have their own e-mail account, personal calendar, and server space. Students are also provided collaborative business software. Teachers made modifications to the business-oriented software to work better in the classroom. Over time, these modifications have become a suite of powerful tools that support the instructional methodology, including shared calendars, discussion boards, document libraries, and evaluation resources. Each project is stored in its own digital briefcase for students to access anytime, anywhere. Teachers can freely share the units with other teachers who can copy, edit, and use them in their own classrooms. Unlike many educational software packages being marketed to traditional schools, our set of tools have grown to specifically support a technology-rich, project-based learning environment.

Many futurists predict that computers will create classrooms without walls and online courses that don't require teachers. New Tech High hasn't abandoned the classroom as the organizational unit of courses, but the classrooms changed in subtly important ways. To begin breaking down the compartmentalization of academic subjects, Language Arts and Social Studies courses were fully integrated into team-taught courses. The teachers share the same classroom with 45 students in a two-hour block that meets each day. In this environment, retreat to traditional approaches is much more difficult. Teachers are forced to rethink how they do things. New Tech also integrated an algebra II and physics course in the same way.

Several other additions were made to the course offerings and graduation requirements designed to support our purpose of creating twenty-first century citizens. New Tech High requires students to take an introductory course called Power Skills in their freshman year. This course gives them some foundation skills in using the technology, learning to manage their time effectively, and learning how to work in groups. These skills are critical for their success in their other classes. The course also helps our students understand themselves. They take an online Myers-Briggs personality assessment, multiple intelligence survey, and a host of other explorations that increase the students' metacognitive awareness of self.

New Tech High also increased the graduation requirements, but not in a way you might expect. In order to graduate, students must take a digital media course, produce a digital portfolio, and complete community service projects and a 50-hour internship. Students must also pass four courses at our local community college, a requirement allowing students to take "elective" courses that, as a small school, we could never offer. It also gives our students valuable experience dealing with the college environment and planning for postsecondary education.

Just as important, being tied to the college forced a change in our school calendar to match the community college's calendar. Now students and teachers could finish the semester courses before an extended winter break. Both come back truly refreshed and ready to start again. At the time, that meant New Tech High started school three weeks before the rest of the district. Today the rest of the district has adopted a calendar similar to New Tech High.

Because the design of New Tech High was sufficiently different from the traditional environment and those differences were institutionalized, the old structures of education that were in conflict with the model were unable to reassert themselves and were instead the targets of further change. As New Tech High evolved, it continued to make more modifications to its schedule. The staff implemented a full block period in all classes to support project-based learning, extended the school day by a few minutes to provide early release days for staff collaboration and curriculum development, and incorporated an advisory period.

Instructional Practice: Learning in Context with Project-Based Learning

With a positive culture in place, a clear purpose defined, and a structure design that would support the vision, the New Tech teachers could now focus on instructional practice that meshed with the other layers of the hierarchy. For the staff, it was about creating a learning environment that mimicked the twenty-first century workplace, which requires communication, collaboration, critical thinking, and effectively using technology. As a member of the teaching team, it was a period of reflection and refinement that I had not experienced since student teaching. Much of my learning was trial and error, but there was also a growing body of research to help me understand how to improve my skills as a teacher.

In the 1960s, research conducted at medical schools revealed a critical flaw in the traditional education paradigm. It showed that although the students were scoring very high on exams, they were unable to diagnose patients. The nation's best students have become very good at selecting the right answer on a multiple-choice question but are often unable to put that knowledge to work in meaningful ways. For example, math students find the correct value for x without knowing what x represents. Economics students define supply and demand without understanding why the street price of cocaine is a possible indicator of the success of police enforcement. Chemistry students make soap after following a teacher-provided recipe and don't know why they did it. At New Tech High, we knew that if our vision for a twenty-first century school were to truly come alive, it was imperative to address what and how students were learning in the classrooms. And because we had tackled the more fundamental needs at the bottom of the hierarchy, we had an environment that was fertile for a different instructional model.

From the early days of New Tech High, we implemented our particular flavor of project and problem-based learning (PBL) in line with what the best learning theory research advocated. While progressive teachers might use projects as a culminating event to their instruction, New Tech teachers use projects as the core of their instructional methodology in all subjects throughout the building. We believe that humans learn best when they have a "need to know." New Tech High teachers start each unit by throwing students into a realistic or real-world project that both engages student interest and generates a list of things the students need to know. Observers will still find teachers lecturing, students completing assignments, and lists of required reading in our classrooms, but each of those activities is used within the context of the project and is timed for when the students are asking for the knowledge.

Because few teacher training programs prepare teachers to work in a twenty-first century school, each New Tech teacher is provided specific and ongoing training to convert state educational standards into engaging, rigorous projects. Experienced teachers have often attained mastery of their subject matter and learned to manage large groups of students, but seldom have they had any experience being a project manager. New Tech teachers must become skilled project managers and learning facilitators to be successful in a project-based classroom. Many experienced teachers who come to work in our school feel like first-year teachers again as they develop new curriculum and relearn how best to deliver it.

Although most teachers experience success in their first year, we have found that it can take as many as three years for a teacher to feel fully proficient in designing PBL projects and guiding the students through them. Once a teacher does become proficient in PBL, few ever go back to the old ways. Teachers find students are more engaged, retain more of what they learn, and are held accountable to their peers to do their best work. In short, the classroom becomes more like a workplace with a culture of professionalism and collaboration. Over the years, our strategy has continually been confirmed by groups of visiting business people. Most recently, a group of Cisco executives commented on how closely our classroom environment resembles their working environment. We couldn't have asked for a better compliment.

Although New Tech High holds its own when it comes to state test scores and outperforms the rest of the district by most measures, it is important to note that we do not prioritize scoring well on the tests as a sole measure of success. One of the worst mixed-messages school leaders often give to teachers is to "be progressive in your instruction" and then turn around and say "we have 143 days to get ready for the state exams." Teachers will never take the leap of faith it requires to implement a PBL methodology if the leadership cannot buffer them from the threat of low test scores. They will quickly retreat to what they know: a teacher-centered curriculum. Similarly, schools that take on the challenge of reform need to be given time to prove themselves. Expecting to see immediate gains in test scores as the school struggles to create the necessary culture for high test scores goes against the theory of the hierarchy.

Integrating twenty-first century skills also meant rethinking how we evaluate students at New Tech High. We soon realized that traditional grades do not provide meaningful feedback on student skills. Even the best grade book software simplifies a student's grade into a single score that gives little information on the particulars of student performance. For example, a student who turns in a major research paper late will often suffer a grade penalty imposed by the teacher. Although it is clear that students should be penalized for turning in late work, when the teacher enters the C+ instead of the B+ into the grade book, the meaningful data evaluating paper quality and work ethic is lost. If a student earns a C in an English class, what does that tell us about the student? Was it a gifted student who did none of the homework but aced every test and paper, or was

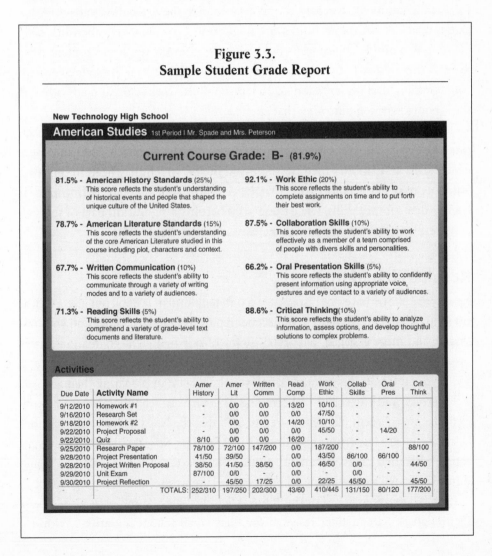

Figure 3.3.
Sample Student Grade Report

New Technology High School

American Studies 1st Period I Mr. Spade and Mrs. Peterson

Current Course Grade: B- (81.9%)

81.5% - American History Standards (25%)
This score reflects the student's understanding of historical events and people that shaped the unique culture of the United States.

78.7% - American Literature Standards (15%)
This score reflects the student's understanding of the core American Literature studied in this course including plot, characters and context.

67.7% - Written Communication (10%)
This score reflects the student's ability to communicate through a variety of writing modes and to a variety of audiences.

71.3% - Reading Skills (5%)
This score reflects the student's ability to comprehend a variety of grade-level text documents and literature.

92.1% - Work Ethic (20%)
This score reflects the student's ability to complete assignments on time and to put forth their best work.

87.5% - Collaboration Skills (10%)
This score reflects the student's ability to work effectively as a member of a team comprised of people with divers skills and personalities.

66.2% - Oral Presentation Skills (5%)
This score reflects the student's ability to confidently present information using appropriate voice, gestures and eye contact to a variety of audiences.

88.6% - Critical Thinking (10%)
This score reflects the student's ability to analyze information, assess options, and develop thoughtful solutions to complex problems.

Activities

Due Date	Activity Name	Amer History	Amer Lit	Written Comm	Read Comp	Work Ethic	Collab Skills	Oral Pres	Crit Think
9/12/2010	Homework #1	-	0/0	0/0	13/20	10/10	-	-	-
9/16/2010	Research Set	-	0/0	0/0	0/0	47/50	-	-	-
9/18/2010	Homework #2	-	0/0	0/0	14/20	10/10	-	-	-
9/22/2010	Project Proposal	-	0/0	0/0	0/0	45/50	-	14/20	-
9/22/2010	Quiz	8/10	0/0	0/0	16/20	-	-	-	-
9/25/2010	Research Paper	78/100	72/100	147/200	0/0	187/200	-	-	88/100
9/28/2010	Project Presentation	41/50	39/50	-	0/0	43/50	86/100	66/100	-
9/28/2010	Project Written Proposal	38/50	41/50	38/50	0/0	46/50	0/0	-	44/50
9/29/2010	Unit Exam	87/100	0/0	-	0/0	-	0/0	-	-
9/30/2010	Project Reflection	-	45/50	17/25	0/0	22/25	45/50	-	45/50
	TOTALS:	252/310	197/250	202/300	43/60	410/445	131/150	80/120	177/200

it a student just learning the English language and, despite rewriting each paper several times, was only able to achieve a C? The traditional transcript tells very little about the student and, for this reason, employers rarely look at them.

New Tech teachers can give multiple grades on that same research paper. They will be likely to score the paper on the academic content, the spelling and grammar, the level of critical thinking, and, finally, on the work ethic, as shown in Figure 3.3. The student who turns the paper in late will be penalized in the work ethic category alone, leaving the other scores to stand on their own. We developed a custom grade book application that allows teachers to enter multiple scores for each assignment. Teachers can also customize the evaluation categories for assignments. For example, homework might only be evaluated in the work ethic column. A multiple-choice test would be assessed in the academic content category. A three-week-long group project would be graded on academic content, collaboration, oral presentation skills, writing skills, work ethic, and any other of the school's learning outcomes that applied.

The New Tech High grade book summarizes all of the student scores in each category separately and gives the student very specific feedback. Students know which skills and abilities they are successful in and which they need to improve. Students now get a report card that reflects how well they are performing in twenty-first century skills. Once these skills become a significant part of the student's evaluation, it changes what we teach and how we teach it.

Results That Matter

New Tech's efforts have not just created a different kind of school, but also a different kind of student. Students in our school report feeling safer, better known, challenged, and more engaged. Our 2005 survey of our first eight graduation classes strongly suggests that students feel New Tech High's use of project-based learning and focus on twenty-first century skills were important in preparing them for college, careers, and citizenship. An amazing 98% of New Tech seniors have a post-secondary enrollment plan, compared to 67% that the Napa Valley Unified School District reports. The report also showed that 96% of New Tech students are very happy with their choice to attend. I am most heartened by the fact that many alumni continue to stop by the school to make sure we are "still doing a good job."

In 2000, representatives of the Bill & Melinda Gates Foundation visited New Tech High as part of their research for their small school initiatives. Within a couple of months, New Technology Foundation, a nonprofit organization set up to support New Tech High and engage in educational reform, received a Bill & Melinda Gates Foundation grant to help other schools replicate the success of the Napa school. The first grant helped the New Tech Foundation create a network of small schools in Northern California based on the New Tech model. In 2004, the New Technology Foundation received a second grant to support additional schools across the country. There are now 24 schools active in the New Tech network and eight new schools coming online in the fall of 2007. New Technology High School continues to host more than 100 visitors each month eager to learn about this small, high-tech, high-touch school. We have committed ourselves to being an active contributor to the ongoing discussions about re-inventing public education. Although we have not solved all the woes facing the 100-year-old system, we have made a significant attempt to create a school for the twenty-first century.

By working with the school district, the business community helped create a vision for a different kind of high school where students were placed in an environment that better reflected the workplace environment. Four years of focus groups, site visitations, and research were invested in New Tech High before it opened. Culturally, its smallness fostered healthier relationships and personalized learning. Its purpose was targeted to focus on twenty-first century skills. Its structures were designed to foster a workplace-like environment and allocate time, people, and resources in a way that supported its purpose. The instruction of traditional academic content was made more relevant through real-world applications. Students worked in teams of their peers every day and had access to technology resources to produce professional products. The result was a significant step in re-inventing the American high school from the ground up—a small school named New Technology High School (NTHS) that has made a big difference in the lives of its students.

Lessons Learned

So what can be learned from New Tech High and its efforts to help others adopt the model? Those who are working to initiate any type of change in instructional practice need to do more than provide minimum training and support to the teachers being asked to implement it. Reformers need to ensure that the systemic and cultural environment will support the changes they are proposing. Although it may look great on paper, taking educational reform "one step at a time" can actually be harder than putting into place a total package of reform that supports a new vision. Systemic reform is difficult to retreat from and has enough momentum to continue through the inevitable rough spots experienced in any change.

In the last five years, the New Technology Foundation has been helping schools replicate the success of New Tech High in school districts across the country. In that time, we've learned a few things about laying the foundation for project-based learning.

- Have a clear reason to make the switch to PBL. For New Tech High, it was incorporating twenty-first century skills. Other schools might use PBL to increase student engagement, address multiple intelligences, or increase critical thinking.

- Commit to PBL as the primary mode of instruction for all classes. Principals who ask for "one project each semester" will never see project-based learning take hold in their school. It all won't fall into place the first year, but without that as a foundation, it is unlikely to ever meet its goals.

- Ensure that the school culture and structure will support PBL. Longer periods, integrated courses, and positive culture all help to foster a change of instructional practice.

- New programs need time to develop and mature; their first year should be considered a benchmark year. Collect data on more than just test scores. Attendance rates, suspension rates, student surveys, and parental involvement can be indicators of success in the lowest levels of the hierarchy.

- Lastly, celebrate your student work. Involving parents and community members in assessing students' products makes the project more authentic and lets them know the amazing things your students are capable of.

Links and Resources

New Technology Foundation, www.newtechfoundation.org

Project-Based Learning, www.bie.org

WestEd, www.wested.org

Partnership for 21st Century Skills, http://www.21stcenturyskills.org

Secretaries Commission on Achieving Necessary Skills, http://wdr.doleta.gov/SCANS/

Myers-Briggs Personality Assessment, http://www.myersbriggs.org/

Multiple Intelligences, http://www.howardgardner.com/

Reflection Questions

1. Does your school ask students to complete academic assignments that integrate content acquisition and skills development with "real challenges" in the larger world?

2. Are all students required to demonstrate proficiency through exhibitions of their work?

3. Teachers who are designing and field testing project-based learning can benefit from faculty meetings at which they present their assignments for critique, guided by common questions:

    a. How does this project reflect adult challenges?

    b. Will the project engage all students?

    c. How well does it integrate disciplinary content and skills?

    d. How compelling is the challenge for each student?

Resources

DiMartino, J., & Clarke, J. (2008). *Personalizing the High School Experience for Each Student*. Alexandria, VA: ASCD.

DiMartino, J., Mangiante, E., & Miles, S. (2006). *High Schools at Work: Creating Student-Centered Learning* (DVDs with facilitator's guide). Alexandria, VA: ASCD.

The George Lucas Educational Foundation, www.edutopia.org

Multiple Intelligences, http://www.howardgardner.com

Myers-Briggs Personality Assessment, http://www.myersbriggs.org

New Technology Foundation, www.newtechfoundation.org

Partnership for 21st Century Skills, http://www.21stcenturyskills.org

Project-Based Learning, www.bie.org

WestEd, www.wested.org

Secretaries Commission on Achieving Necessary Skills, http://wdr.doleta.gov/SCANS

Instruction

Making Learning Personal

Ron Newell and Mark Van Ryzin

Minnesota New Country School, Henderson, Minnesota

How can a school personalize the learning experience? For most of us who attended a comprehensive high school, minimal opportunity for personalization was encountered, often in extracurricular experiences or as part of a team. But personalizing curriculum and self-pacing are concepts that are now embedded in practice in a unique innovative school: the Minnesota New Country School, located in the small town of Henderson, Minnesota.

Let us consider one student's experience. Ben is a senior at the Minnesota New Country School (MNCS). He first enrolled at the school in tenth grade, making 2006–2007 his third year at the school. Ben left his other school and enrolled at MNCS because he was frustrated with his treatment by students and staff members at the comprehensive high school he previously attended; basically, he felt ignored and "put down." Ben has a slight speech impediment; he stutters when he speaks, but over the last three years he has overcome much of the fear of conversing with peers and adults.

Ben feels he is treated differently at MNCS. He is considered an individual in all aspects. Ben has been able to meet state standards by creating personal, interdisciplinary projects rather than going to classes. Starting with his interests, he works with his "advisor" on developing projects that will be relevant to his interests and to his needs to meet state curricular guidelines.

In his second year at MNCS, Ben did a project on Native American tribes. His advisor Dee directed him to another advisor on staff that had expertise in history and social studies and provided meaningful resources, including print, media, and Internet, to complete the project. Dee also helped Ben define and refine his project to meet state standards in history and culture. Via the Internet and other resources, he was able to find Native American tribal elders with whom he could meet and talk. He was also able to obtain resources with the direction of the school media director, Mary Ann, through an interlibrary loan system.

Ben accomplished his Native American tribes project in approximately 100 hours. He accomplished many additional projects that met other expected curricular areas. By doing projects that were of interest to him at the time, Ben was able to meet the standards outlined by the state that were expected for a high school education.

What active role does an advisor play in helping Ben learn what he needs to learn? Ben reports that his advisor checks in with him daily and confers with him about his projects. Dee also gives him feedback with encouraging words or with suggestions. Dee uses data from standardized tests to learn Ben's capabilities. From working with Ben and his parents on his Personal Learning Plan, Dee has determined what are Ben's interests, goals, strengths, and weaknesses.

Each member of the staff at MNCS helped Ben learn the process and provided resources or consulted with him to refine his ideas. For each project, Ben is required to find three types of resources (a live person, print sources, and Internet resources). The advisor and one other licensed advisor will serve on his proposal and assessment committee. Another advisor and possibly a paraprofessional in the learning community, or from the outer community (a community expert), will round out his assessment team.

Advisors help Ben meet state standards by suggesting resources that are within his ability to understand and that challenge him. Also, advisors or committee members will ask challenging questions of him that will help deepen his thinking about the project and possibly broaden the project into meeting other course standards.

Ben meets face-to-face with his advisor either one-on-one or in an advisory meeting on a daily basis. Sometimes a project he initiates will become a group or partnership project with another student with a similar idea or interest. Advisors will make suggestions of that nature to bring like-minded students together to do projects. Students at MNCS must do projects both alone and with others to meet graduation requirements.

Ben can meet state standards in all curricular areas through interest-driven projects with advisor guidance, and he also will learn skills that will contribute to his becoming a good college student or worker. Ben says that the process he goes through at MNCS improves his organization skills and helps him become more responsible. He has learned to manage information and solve problems. He feels that he is better prepared for college and life as a result of the process at MNCS.

When asked whether some students were treated differently, Ben responded in the affirmative. But he stated that that is a good thing. Each student is at a different place, doing projects that are interest-driven, and they are working toward graduation at their own pace. Consequently he would not expect that each student would be treated the same. But that doesn't mean that students are treated unfairly; just the opposite. Being treated fairly and being treated the same are not synonymous at this school.

How different is this school from others Ben attended? He said that his previous school experiences were not interesting, especially when he was forced to do the same things as everyone else. He found that boring. He is doing much better at MNCS; he was convinced that he was not a good learner prior to coming to MNCS, and now he feels that he can accomplish whatever he wants. "This school has been a perfect fit for me," said Ben. "I knew what I wanted to do, and I can still tie it into state standards. School is now more interesting and more fun."

Ben is currently working on his senior project. The senior project requires 300 to 400 hours of work and a 30-minute presentation. The presentation is the final exhibit of Ben's portfolio, and he must meet certain standards in the exhibition in order to graduate. Ben's senior project is about charter schools and how they are different and what makes them successful. He has met with legislators and even has testified at legislative committees. For a young man who had to overcome a fear of public speaking, Ben indeed has come along way!

The Process

The process that allows for personalizing instruction includes an online project management system that leads students through the project process. First Ben has to brainstorm an idea and find how it may meet state standards. A drop-down menu allows Ben to see the standards and curricular areas that are needed, and which ones he has not yet met. His advisor helps him refine the search by making suggestions to look under other curricular areas. For example, his Native-American project not only met standards in American history, but also in sociology and human cultures. There are also the means of exhibiting what Ben learns; standards in the curricular areas of speaking, writing, art, or language may be met with a project product or presentation.

After refining his set of questions so that they may meet a variety of standards, Ben does a task analysis. For example, he will brainstorm what resources may be available (see above), then he will use his hours during the day to find, read, and analyze what he needs to complete the project. He has to log the hours he spends on this project and others on a daily basis. Ben also must keep a journal daily regarding how his projects are progressing, what barriers he met, what problems he may have had with resources, and so forth. He must balance his work on this project with other projects he is currently undertaking. Often students at MNCS are developing three to eight projects simultaneously, and they must manage their time accordingly.

The project management system allows the advisor entry into each student's project documentation of time and learning, as well as daily journals; yet there is still time for advisors to meet face-to-face with each of their 18 advisees during the week. Because each of their students may be working on different portions of the state-wide curricula at different times and in different ways, the process of advisement becomes much more complicated. Advisors do less instructing in factual information and more on processes of acquiring purposeful information that make sense in a project. When state standards are taken into consideration, the project becomes more meaningful and either deeper or more broad. It is the job of the advisor to ask meaningful questions ("essential questions") that lead the student to an in-depth project that meets the standards of knowledge and skills in a variety of disciplines.

The online project management system also allows for students to assess themselves on life skills. In some cases the student creates his rubric upon which the project is assessed. Because the project requires more than one adult from the learning community (and sometimes from outside the immediate school population) the student obtains feedback from a number of adults. The assessment committee, usually the same persons who made up the proposal committee, meets with the student when the project is completed. The student defends his learning, with his advisor functioning as an advocate and the other adults as assessors. Project credits are then assigned and standards are checked off a master list.

Providing a personalized experience for Ben and other students could not be done if the school used the old time-based, curriculum-based approach. When school is organized around classroom teaching and learning, as it is in most schools, teachers have difficulty personalizing, and students are less valued as individuals. The curriculum coverage usually is placed at the forefront; student needs, especially different pacing for learning and anything of interest, gives way to the curriculum organized into classrooms organized into specific time slots. By freeing teachers from classrooms and lesson delivery, MNCS makes it possible for teachers to advise and coach individuals, one student at a time.

As students move through this system, meeting course standards via personal projects, they acquire skills well beyond state standards in knowledge and skills. Students learn to analyze, think critically, problem solve, organize, and relate to adults. By following the process of personalized, interest-driven, project-based learning, adolescents become productive adults, ready for college or work. Additional outcomes are met by the project approach, outcomes that are difficult to deliver by the classroom method.

Why Personalize Instruction?

Personalizing for each student is the key to engagement in education. Why? According to constructivist theory, how we construct knowledge depends upon what the learner already knows. What the learner already knows depends on the kinds of experiences that they had, how the learner has organized those experiences into knowledge structures, and the beliefs used to interpret objects and events encountered in the world. Constructivists claim that we construct our own reality through interpreting experiences in the world. The teacher cannot imprint his or her interpretation onto the learner, as we attempt to do with curriculum-driven teaching, because teacher and students do not share a set of common experiences and interpretations.

Rather, reality resides to some degree in the mind of each learner, who interprets the external world according to his or her own experiences, beliefs, and knowledge. We each therefore conceive of the external world somewhat differently, based upon our unique set of experiences with the world and our beliefs about those experiences.

Constructivist models strive to create environments in which learners actively participate in the environment in ways that are intended to help them construct their own knowledge, rather than having the teacher interpret the world and ensure that students understand the world as she does. In constructivist environments learners are actively engaged in interpreting the external world and reflecting on their interpretations. This is "active learning" in the sense that learners must participate and interact with the surrounding environment in order to create their own view of the subject.

A constructivist process is concerned with designing environments that support the construction of knowledge. These environments require internal negotiation, a process of articulating mental models, using those models to explain, predict, and infer, and reflecting on their utility. They also require social negotiation, a process of sharing a reality with others by using processes the same or similar to those used in internal negotiation. A constructivist learning community would offer exploration of real-world environments, processes that are regulated by each individual's intentions, needs, expectations, or all three. The experiences ought to be meaningful, authentic contexts for learning, which have been derived from and situated in the real world and based on authentic real-life practice.

Constructivist theory is backed by brain research. According to Caine & Caine (1998), brain research shows that there are three conditions to be met if a learning experience is truly brain compatible: a state of "relaxed alertness," an "orchestrated immersion" in complex activity, and "active processing" of the experience through reflection. A state of relaxed alertness is fostered by the following:

- A setting that supports group work and private study
- An environment that is lighthearted and not depressing
- Competence and quality are recognized and endorsed
- Students help one another with projects and concepts
- Flexible space is used as a way to introduce interesting changes in the physical environment
- Technology is used to enhance learning
- Teachers and other staff support one another
- Relevant connections are made between course concepts (economics) and school activities (fund raising)
- School priorities reflect curriculum goals
- School happens inside and outside the classroom

Orchestrated immersion is characterized by the following:

- Evidence of student involvement, creativity, and enjoyment
- Many different moods, including playfulness and serious thought
- Students asking questions or making observations that link content to life
- Personal life themes, metaphors, interests, and dreams being engaged
- Students persevere with projects or return to them without being reminded
- There are signs of positive collaboration that persists beyond the school day
- Students persevere to overcome difficulties in understanding or communication
- Students suggest relevant projects of their own

Active processing of events occurs when students

- Examine their own performance and results
- Seek feedback and advice from others
- Compare work with others
- Test concepts and procedures, perhaps pushing the boundaries of what is typically done
- Engage in some research for facts, information, and relevant history of topics they themselves choose
- Seek help from teachers and other students with understanding and development of projects
- Seek assistance for improvement

The theory and research described mirror exactly what MNCS has been able to do with the project-based, advisory-based learning program. By creating an interest-driven approach rather than a curriculum-driven approach, constructivist theory and brain research are programmatically manifested. By having students negotiate with advisors and peers, students come to an awareness of their own thinking process and problem-solving methods. In addition, they learn to collaborate and negotiate, which are communication skills needed for the twenty-first century.

Lynn Stoddard (2004) mentions three basic needs of pre-adolescents and adolescents: the needs to have their *identity* respected and valued, to have daily *interaction,* and for natural *inquiry* to take place. If a school could be built around these three elements, it would become a personalized school. The time-based, curriculum-based method we adopted over the last 150 years in American education does not allow for the respect of individual identity, student-to-student and student-to-teacher interaction, or student-directed inquiry. Hence, school is something most adolescent participants have difficulty with, although many appear to function fairly well within the system.

But the modern adolescent no longer sees the value of being subservient to an archaic system. Too many are falling through the cracks, either by not graduating or doing poorly. As a result, Alternative Learning Centers, home-schooling, charters, and private schools proliferate. According to Stoddard, if schools could build in practices that value identity, interaction, and inquiry, hence personalization, they would have happier and more productive students. It appears that MNCS, by instituting the practices mentioned, has institutionalized respecting identity, interaction, and personal inquiry.

The ASCD Yearbook for 1999 included an article by Brian J. Caldwell, called "Education for the Public Good: Strategic Intentions for the 21st Century," in which he outlined eight concepts that schools of the future would utilize:

- *Life-long learning,* the view that learning is a pleasurable activity, inspiring people to wish to continually learn, rather than the force-fed, curriculum-based, time-based compulsory education method that made learning a drudgery

- *Learner-driven-learning,* learning that extends beyond adolescence, using technologies beyond teachers and school buildings, that develops from student interest

- *Just-in-time learning,* the notion that the best learning opportunities are created when interest and motivation are at their peak, which can happen at any time of the day

- *Transformative learning,* or learning that changes attitudes, aspirations, values, and beliefs and brings a higher sense of purpose and productivity than before the education intervention

- *Collaborative learning,* or using technology to shift individualistic modes of learning and doing to collaborative means of learning and doing, thus allowing teams of students and adults to collaborate regardless of geographic location

- *Contextual learning,* which posits that learning is more effective when it is connected to relevant, real-world experiences

- *Learning-to-learn,* or gaining the skills that allow people to learn what they need or want to learn, at any time.

Caldwell's view was optimistically written in the late 1990s, when technology and global economies began making great changes in the workplace and in the marketplace. Educators attempted many reforms since then, but very few schools adopted Caldwell's list in full—except for MNCS.

The founders of MNCS incorporated all of these futuristic learning scenarios into the flexible learning program. By abandoning the time-based, curriculum-driven, classroom delivery–oriented methodology of the previous century, MNCS developed a program that was able to accommodate all of the learning concepts in the preceding list. Futurists and farsighted educators saw the possibilities for personalizing education. The Minnesota New Country School put the ideas into practice and proved they can work.

To place personalization at the forefront of education requires drastically changing the learning community. It requires a great deal of risk on the part of educators to remake the entire program. Falling back on the old behaviorist classroom model is the easy way; by adopting the learner-driven project-based model, educators change the paradigm of what it means to be a student, what it means to be a teacher, the adult-to-student relationships, the adult-to-adult relationships, and even the student-to-student relationships.

Research Supporting the Personalized Approach

Traditional secondary schools do not have a sterling track record when it comes to motivating and engaging students in learning. In fact, students' preference for challenge, curiosity, and focus on independent mastery have all been found to decrease steadily over time, with an especially large drop during the transition from elementary to middle school (Harter, 1981). A similar decline is found in student engagement (Marks, 2000), motivation (Eccles, Midgley, & Adler, 1984; Gottfried, Fleming, & Gottfried, 2001), commitment to school (Epstein & McPartland, 1976), and the perceived quality of school life (Hirsch & Rapkin, 1987).

Research shows that by high school many students have lost interest in school and find classes to be boring (Harter, 1981; Steinberg, Brown, & Dornbusch, 1996). This lack of interest is reflected in reduced attention and effort in school, as well as widespread cheating on homework and tests (Josephson Institute of Ethics, 2002; Schab, 1991; Steinberg et al., 1996). With these developments come the expected declines in academic achievement. This gradual process of disengagement culminates in dropping out of school before graduation for as many as *half a million adolescents* each year (National Center for Education Statistics, 2001), a truly staggering total.

Unfortunately, these troubles come at a particularly critical time, given that adolescence is when psychological disturbances emerge, such as anxiety, eating disorders, and depression (Kazdin, 1993). Further, adolescents show an increase in the frequency of high-risk behaviors, such as misbehavior in school, cigarette, alcohol, or hard drug use, and teenage pregnancy (Dryfoos, 1990).

These motivational, emotional, and behavioral problems are often reciprocally related and mutually reinforcing (Roeser, Eccles, & Sameroff, 2000; Roeser, Eccles, Sameroff, & Strobel, 1998). A downward trajectory in school can have a negative effect on other areas of a student's life. Cumulatively, these types of problems in adolescence can inhibit intellectual growth and emotional maturation and impede the transition to adulthood, resulting in not only individual-level effects such as lower earning capacity and increased likelihood of unemployment and poverty, but also significant social costs in terms of reduced productivity and increased expenditures for welfare programs and law enforcement (*Great Transitions,* 1995).

Adolescence is a uniquely critical time in human development. The events that transpire during this time can have implications for the individual that extend far beyond the teenage years, as well as implications for the health and welfare of society. As a major component of the adolescent life experience, secondary schools can provide a strong platform for future success *or* can solidify negative attitudes and self-concepts for life. Clearly, if we could change the negative aspects of high school, we could positively affect many lives.

Unfortunately, evaluating schools solely in terms of test scores often fails to reveal the true nature of the learning environment and how that environment contributes to adolescent mental health and adjustment. A school that makes adequate yearly progress on standardized test scores while contributing to the frustration, apathy, loneliness, and alienation of many of its students cannot be considered a success.

What is needed is a means by which schools can be assessed as cultures that create a set of relationships, norms of behaviors, values, and commitments that lead to the development of healthy and productive students. According to psychological theory (Ryan & Deci, 2000; Eccles et al., 1993), school environments can achieve this objective by providing for students' basic psychological needs: autonomy (choice, self-management), belongingness (strong teacher and peer relationships), and competence (equal opportunity to succeed on one's own terms, emphasis on deep understanding, and recognition of effort). Students in these sorts of supportive environments respond by engaging more directly in their learning and, over time, gaining confidence in themselves as achievers. In applying this theory to secondary schools, researchers have found that traditional middle and high school environments are often unable to meet the developmental needs of adolescents; in turn, this increases the risk of negative motivational, behavioral, and emotional outcomes, such as those already highlighted (Eccles & Midgley, 1989; Roeser, Eccles, & Sameroff, 1998; Roeser, Eccles, Sameroff, & Strobel, 1998).

For example, research has found that middle school environments typically offer fewer opportunities for students to exercise choice in the classroom (Eccles et al., 1993; Feldlaufer, Midgley, & Eccles, 1988; Midgley & Feldlaufer, 1987) and exhibit more controlling behavior by teachers (Eccles et al., 1993). During this transition, students also experience a reduced perception of teacher support, fewer opportunities for interaction and cooperation with peers, and less positive student–teacher relationships (Midgley, Feldlaufer, & Eccles, 1989). Also, the transition to secondary school often brings with it changes in task organization, such as more whole-class instruction, increased ability grouping and public evaluations, and a greater emphasis on grades and competition, which can limit the opportunities that students have to feel competent (Eccles et al., 1984; Eccles et al., 1993).

Lessons Learned: Applying the Research at MNCS

The Minnesota New Country School has endeavored to offer a supportive adolescent environment by creating a democratic learning community characterized by a student body of less than 120 and advisory groupings of 17 to 18 students. The school offers students a friendly, open, supportive environment in which to grow. Students are valued, and deep interpersonal relationships are desired. The setting is highly personalized and responsive to each student's goals and needs. Each student's uniqueness and learning styles are taken into account, so that each student's identity is highly valued.

This personalization would not be possible without a physical setting conducive to support of advisories, personal work spaces, specialty break-out rooms, and "flexible-use space." The New Country School staff know that in order to build a school that helps adolescent psychological development, autonomy, belongingness and a positive goal orientation must be supported. The learning program and the physical space of the building do just that. By creating an innovative and positive environment, the Minnesota New Country School fulfills the psychological needs of adolescents by creating the physical and intellectual space necessary for growth.

We know this from three years of studies that show that MNCS and other schools like it are actually growing engagement and hope because they have high degrees of perceived autonomy, belongingness, and mastery goal orientation. The Hope Study, which links autonomy, belongingness, mastery goal orientation, and engagement to dispositional growth in hope, has evidence that MNCS has been able to build high levels of hope in students who came with low levels of hope. A healthy hope index level is a psychological attribute that has a high correlation to resilience, persistence, and success in life. The learning program, primarily made up of interest-driven projects and full-time advisories, proves to be a healthy environment for adolescents to thrive in.

The reason Ben, whose story we related at the beginning of the chapter, and so many other students have become successful is apparent: personalizing for every student allows each and every adolescent to feel valued, allows them to learn at their own pace, and gives them ownership of the complete educational enterprise. Reorganizing how teachers relate to students and to each other allows for high levels of personal support and a positive goal orientation.

Personalizing education for adolescents is possible. The Minnesota New Country School has a proven, personalized, project-based approach that can be an example for others to follow.

Bibliography

Brown, B., Steinberg, L., & Dornbusch, S. (1996). *Beyond the classroom: Why school reform has failed and what parents should do.* New York: Simon & Schuster.

Caine, R., & Caine, G. (1998). *Unleashing the power of perceptual change: The promise of brain based teaching.* Alexandria, VA: ASCD.

Caldwell, B. J. (1999). Education for the public good: Strategic intentions for the 21st century. In D. D. Marsh (ed.), *Preparing our schools for the 21st century* (ch. 3). Alexandria, VA: ASCD.

Deci, E. L., Nezlek, J., & Sheinman, L. (1981). Characteristics of the rewarder and intrinsic motivation of the rewardee. *Journal of Personality and Social Psychology, 40,* 1–10.

Deci, E. L., Schwartz, A. J., Sheinman, L., & Ryan, R. M. (1981). An instrument to access adults' orientations toward control versus autonomy with children: Reflections on intrinsic motivation and perceived competence. *Journal of Educational Psychology, 73,* 642–650.

Dryfoos, J. G. (1990). *Adolescents at risk: Prevalence and prevention.* New York: Oxford University Press.

Eccles, J. S., & Midgley, C. (1989). Stage/environment fit: Developmentally appropriate classrooms for early adolescents. In R. E. Ames & C. Ames (Eds.), *Research on motivation in education* (Vol. 3, pp. 139–186). San Diego, CA: Academic Press.

Eccles, J., Midgley, C., & Adler, T. (1984). Grade-related changes in the school environment: Effects of achievement motivation. In J. G. Nicholls (Ed.), *The development of achievement motivation* (pp. 283–331). Greenwich, CT: JAI Press.

Eccles, J. S., Wigfield, A., Midgley, C., Reuman, D., MacIver, D., & Feldlaufer, H. (1993). Negative effects of traditional middle schools on students' motivation. *The Elementary School Journal, 93,* 553–574.

Epstein, J. L., & McPartland, J. M. (1976). The concept and measurement of the quality of school life. *American Educational Research Journal, 13,* 15–30.

Feldlaufer, H., Midgley, C., & Eccles, J. (1988). Student, teacher, and observer perceptions of the classroom before and after the transition to junior high school. *Journal of Early Adolescence, 8,* 133–156.

Gottfried, A. E., Fleming, J. S., & Gottfried, A. W. (2001). Continuity of academic intrinsic motivation from childhood through late adolescence: A longitudinal study. *Journal of Educational Psychology, 93,* 3–13.

Great Transitions: Preparing Adolescents for a New Century (concluding report of the Carnegie Council on Adolescent Development) (1995). New York: Carnegie Corporation.

Harter, S. (1981). A new self-report scale of intrinsic versus extrinsic orientation in the classroom: Motivational and informational components. *Developmental Psychology, 17,* 300–312.

Hirsch, B. J., & Rapkin, B. D. (1987). The transition to junior high school: A longitudinal study of self-esteem, psychological symptomatology, school life, and social support. *Child Development, 58,* 1235–1243.

Josephson Institute of Ethics, 2002; accessed online at http://charactercounts .org/programs/reportcard/2002/index.html

Kazdin, A. E. (1993). Adolescent mental health: Prevention and treatment programs. *American Psychologist, 48,* 127–141.

Marks, H. M. (2000). Student engagement in instructional activity: Patterns in the elementary, middle and high school years. *American Educational Research Journal, 37,* 153–184.

Midgley, C., & Feldlaufer, H. (1987). Students' and teachers' decision-making fit before and after the transition to junior high school. *Journal of Early Adolescence, 7,* 225–241.

Midgley, C., Feldlaufer, H., & Eccles, J. S. (1989). Student/teacher relations and attitudes toward mathematics before and after the transition to junior high school. *Child Development, 60,* 981–992.

National Center for Education Statistics, 2001; accessed online at http://nces .ed.gov/Pubsearch/pubsinfo.asp?pubid=2002130.

Newell, R. J. (2003). *Passion for learning: How project-based learning meets the needs of 21st-century students.* Lanham, MD: Scarecrow Press.

Newell, R. J., & Van Ryzin, M. J. (2007). Growing hope as a measure of school effectiveness. *Phi Delta Kappan, 88,* 465–471.

Roeser, R. W., Eccles, J. S., & Sameroff, A. J. (2000). School as a context of social-emotional development: A summary of research findings. *Elementary School Journal, 100,* 443–471.

Roeser, R. W., Eccles, J. S., Sameroff, A. J., & Strobel, K. R. (1998). Linking the study of schooling and mental health: Selected issues and empirical illustrations at the level of the individual. *Educational Psychologist, 33,* 153–176.

Roeser, R. W., Midgley, C., & Urdan, T. C. (1996). Perceptions of the school psychological environment and early adolescents' psychological and behavioral functioning in school: The mediating role of goals and belonging. *Journal of Educational Psychology, 88,* 408–422.

Ryan, R., & Deci, E. (2000). Self-determination theory and the facilitation of intrinsic motivation, social development, and well-being. *American Psychologist, 55,* 68–78.

Schab, F. (1991). Schooling without learning: Thirty years of cheating in high school. *Adolescence, 26,* 839–847.

Steinberg, L., Brown, B., & Dornbusch, S. (1996). *Beyond the classroom: Why school reform has failed and what parents need to do.* New York: Simon and Schuster.

Stoddard, L. (2004). *Educating for human greatness.* Brandon, VT: Holistic Education Press.

Reflection Questions

1. What opportunities exist at your school for all students to engage in deep learning on subjects that are of interest to them?

2. Is there a project management system in place in your school that allows teachers to track the progress and assess student learning on individual projects?

3. How would engaging in the kind of personalized teaching and learning practices the authors describe improve learning outcomes for students in your school?

4. How can personalized learning be placed front and center on your school's agenda?

Resources

The Big Picture Company, www.bigpicture.org

Breaking Ranks: A Field Guide for Leading Change. (2008). Alexandria, VA: NASSP.

Clarke, J., & DiMartino, J. (2009). Personalized teaching. *Virginia Journal of Education, 102*(5).

DiMartino, J., & Clarke, J. (2008). *Personalizing the High School Experience for Each Student.* Alexandria, VA: ASCD.

DiMartino, J., Clarke, J., & Wolk, D. (eds.) (2003). *Personalized Learning: Preparing High School Students to Create Their Futures.* Lanham, MD: Rowman & Littlefield.

EdVisions Schools, www.edvisions.com

Newell, R. (2003). *Passion for Learning: How Project-Based Learning Meets the Needs of 21st-Century Students.* Lanham, MD: Rowman & Littlefield.

Assessment

Deepening Intellectual Curiosity by Using Exhibitions as Alternative Assessments

Catherine DeLaura

School of the Future, New York, New York

New York State is under the mandate of severe, high-stakes testing requiring that a student take and pass between five to seven regents exams in English, math, history, science, and foreign language in order to graduate from a New York State high school with a Regents diploma. School of the Future (SOF), a small public 6–12 Coalition of Essential Schools (CES) member located in Gramercy Park in Manhattan, is part of the New York State Performance Standards Consortium that has a waiver from the Regents testing. Consortium schools do alternative assessments instead of the regents exams.

The New York State Performance Standards Consortium is a coalition of high schools from across New York State that has developed a system of rigorous commencement-level performance-based assessment tasks that exceed the New York State Regents standards. In 1991 a group of small secondary schools were recognized by former New York State Commissioner of Education Dr. Tom Sobol as model schools. Several of these schools had developed models of alternative assessment, and Dr. Sobol granted the schools a waiver from the state exams. There are several underlying assumptions concerning the exhibition policy in general. According to Jill Davidson, editor of the CES magazine *Horace*, "Exhibitions are performance-based assessments made visible, public demonstrations of mastery that depend on participation of people from outside the school community as mentors and evaluators" (Davidson, 2007, p. 2).

In 1995 when Richard Mills became state commissioner he changed the state's testing policy in favor of high-stakes testing for all schools. The fight to protect the waiver started in 1998 when the New York State Performance Standards Consortium was formed by members of the Compact for Learning schools and CES. Teachers, parents, and schools organized to regain the waiver that was being threatened.

The Consortium is not against testing, but against high-stakes testing. SOF prepares students for the SAT exams and teachers give classroom tests. Tests are just one indicator of mastery, not the only indicator as is the case with the high-stakes regents exams that most New York State students must pass to graduate. Under Mills, the Consortium schools were slowly losing the waiver. When I came to SOF in 2002, we had technically lost the waiver and the regents exams were being slowly added in. We prepared students for all five exams from 2003 to 2005. With very little test prep, the students did well. Our passing rates for the Math A, Living Environment, and Global and U.S. History exams were over 90% the first time they took the exam. But the pressure of doing both regents exams and the exhibitions was not making school a meaningful experience for the students. Tailoring ourselves to two assessment systems was wasting valuable instructional time and could not be sustained. In June 2005 we regained an extension of the waiver for several more years. The state was unwilling to agree to a permanent waiver. The legislation passed by the New York State Legislature stated that since Consortium schools needed more time to prepare their schools to give the exam that the waiver would be extended until 2011. We are grateful for any break from the mandate, but we are still working with the state to fully regain the regents' waiver.

Developing the Exhibition Process at the School of the Future

The School of the Future opened in 1990 as part of an Apple Education grant. Kathy Pelles assumed the principalship in 1991 and developed SOF as a CES school. Our students are drawn from all over the city. Throughout the 1990s we developed the exhibition process. By being clear in our mission we have been able to attract students and parents who are committed to our alternative assessment. Our parents have vocally and passionately supported the waiver to the regents and were active in the Consortium to re-win the waiver in 2005. Time

Out From Testing, an organization formed by a Consortium parent, fights high-stakes testing citywide (www.timeoutfromtesting.org). Without their support, we would not have been able to maintain our alternative system. Beth Wood, the mother of a member of the graduating class of 2007, said, "The exhibition process allowed my son, who is not a good standardized test taker, to choose topics to explore that interested him within the range of core subjects over his four high school years, instead of cramming for final exit exams. He would not have been successful at a more traditional school and he has just been accepted to the college of his dreams."

I came to SOF in 2002 as the assistant principal of the high school. The School of the Future appealed to me for its commitment to preparing students for the real world. The CES Common Principles were evident throughout the school from scheduling to instructional vision to democratic practices. We operate very autonomously within the department of education and we used this freedom to be innovative and creative and allow students to learn to think critically in this era of high-stakes testing.

Kathy Pelles left the following year to assume a new supervisory position formed under Chancellor Joel Klein. Michael Bloomberg was taking mayoral control of New York City schools and this was the first in a series of major reorganizations that have transformed public education in New York City. I assumed the role of principal in the summer of 2003. That was the first year of the CES Small Schools project. We pushed off applying for the project until 2004. We wanted to make sure the new leadership had more experience to support mentoring a new small school.

Using Exhibitions to Deepen Learning Experiences

My focus for SOF over the past five years has been to document the distributive leadership, sharpen the instructional vision, and strengthen the student voice in the school. I aspire for all students to have choice. Young people who are well-skilled in the academic subjects can decide what they want to pursue after high school. I don't want any students deciding to not pursue college because they can't do the work. Building social and academic responsibility is a main focus of our mission. We have strived to make that true inside and outside of the classroom. We have increased student involvement in hiring, the school leadership team, student-run classes, and involvement in community service, such as school and roof clean-up days and the AIDS Walk. Students have accompanied staff to numerous CES Institutes around the country to present about the school and learn about student involvement in other schools. We have developed French and Spanish language exchange trips to two schools in Southern France and Spain. Authentic, real-world experiences have greatly improved our program.

At SOF, we use exhibitions in place of standardized testing. Our ethnically, socioeconomically, and academically diverse high school students take the English Language Arts Regents Exam and complete four exhibitions to obtain a New York State Regents Diploma. The exhibition process reflects the kind of deep teaching and learning for which we strive. Students complete one exhibition each year while they are in grades nine through twelve at the School of the Future. Students must complete two exhibitions in humanities (including history, English, and foreign language), one in math, and one in science. The exhibitions require students to demonstrate analytic thinking, research writing skills, mathematical computation and problem-solving skills, and scientific thinking skills. Students are asked to demonstrate intellectual accomplishment by constructing knowledge, engaging in inquiry, and making connections to the world beyond school.

A Student Perspective: Eric's Story

It is a common misconception that the exhibition process is merely a way around the regents examinations, a clever technique by progressives to mask a lack of academic motivation in the public school system. I have told my friends, most of whom attend schools with a heavy emphasis on standardized testing, about this new and innovative process. The most common reactions have been jealousy, followed by an uneducated assessment of how absurd it is to write a paper instead of being tested on what you have learned. However, as someone who has passed two regents exams before I attended SOF, I can honestly say that exhibitions are, if anything, more difficult, and infinitely more useful.

When I first attended SOF as a freshman, I was accustomed to the traditional test-taking process. When I discovered that I had to write a paper on math in order to graduate, I was more than a little disturbed. I asked myself, "What's the point, when I could just as easily fill in little bubbles on an answer key?" Regardless of my opinion, I realized I would be held to the same strict standards as everyone else, and that there was nothing to gain by putting it off.

Before I could get started, I had to learn the basics of the exhibition process. The first step was to choose one of three "EQs," or essential questions, which needed to be answered by a well-thought-out thesis. I chose: "How can we relate ratios to the real world?" After consulting my teacher so he could ascertain that my thesis was acceptable, I didn't have any time to waste before getting started on my first draft. This was a painful process, and seemed impossible. Little did I know, I was approaching the task the wrong way, as my advisor informed me upon seeing my well-written, but decidedly un-mathematical paper.

Although the exhibition needed to be in the form of a research paper, that was no excuse for straying away from mathematical formulas. My work over the next few weeks involved scouring familiar surroundings for evidence of ratios. It wasn't long before I started applying math to the real world; the same math that I hear my regent-taking friends calling "useless" and not relevant.

On a family trip to Costa Rica, I examined the map and utilized conversion factors (a kind of ratio) to compare it to the real world. I also drew upon the recent elections for inspiration, going in depth on the different voting systems, all of which involved ratios of some kind. The last part of my paper detailed how ratios are applied to business financial management. All of these topics had been covered in math class in one way or another throughout the year, so it wasn't like the exhibition took priority over our schoolwork. Rather, they were the ultimate test of not only our memorization of facts, but our understanding of the material. Students who didn't pay attention in class did poorly on their exhibitions, in contrast to the regents, where a little bit of cramming a week before the test guarantees a good grade.

I won't lie and say the research made me love math, because it didn't. However, there is no denying that applying (arguably) dry concepts to the world is infinitely more engaging than filling out bubbles in a test booklet.

(Continued)

More important, I remember much of what I researched for my exhibition, which is saying a lot for someone who has difficulty in math.

My sophomore exhibition, a historical research paper, was a completely different experience. This time around, we were given a lot more freedom in terms of choosing our topic. I have always been an avid reader, film-watcher and gamer. Because of the pleasure I derived from these activities, censorship was something that got me angry. Our class discussions on similar practices in countries such as Nazi Germany and Communist Russia led me to the conclusion that this was the perfect topic for my paper. Not only was it relevant to the curriculum, but also something of great interest to me. I crafted an essential question and a thesis, and with my teacher's approval, began to write.

After handing in the first of many drafts (read by a teacher I didn't know, to avoid bias), I was told my paper lacked structure and organization. My sponsor, Mr. Copeland, suggested that I organize my ideas in a special format. What was previously a well written, yet disorganized paper, was fast turning into something I could be proud of. After many hours of hard work and guidance, I was finally ready to work on my presentation, which was arguably more difficult than the writing.

I began by reading through my essay and picking out all the crucial facts. We had many different choices of presentation, from video clips and music to billboards with illustrations. I chose a PowerPoint presentation, which was simple thanks to School of the Future's supply of technology. I didn't sleep much before the night of my presentation. I wished things were as simple as sitting down and taking a test. Instead, I had to present in front of a panel of judges, consisting of teachers, as well as my peers. I was called to present after every member stated their individual grades and reached a consensus. Quivering nervously, struggling to ignore the butterflies in my stomach, I began to speak. Despite the obviously high pressure to succeed, everyone on the panel was supportive and encouraging as I made my argument. Once I was finished, they asked me to step into the hallway while they graded my presentation. After what seemed like an eternity, I was allowed back in to hear the verdict. I must have literally let out a sigh of relief when I found out my grade: an MD, or mastery with distinction (the equivalent of an A+).

Using Rubrics to Measure Student Success

Each year students choose the subject area they would like to explore for that year. Their subject area teacher becomes their sponsor for the exhibition. The faculty sponsor acts as the student's coach, the equivalent of a research advisor, providing academic and emotional support throughout the process. Students are expected to produce a paper much like a college thesis that documents their research, as well as to present this work in front of a committee of teachers, peers, and community members. The student's exhibition project is evaluated based on an established rubric based on the Habits of Mind, which were developed by veteran school reformer Ted Sizer and the CES. Exhibitions can consist of a historical research paper, foreign language research paper, literary criticism paper, original work, a science experiment, or applied mathematics. They are guided by an essential question that allows the student to explore the five Habits of Mind: point of view, evidence, connections, significance, and alternative point of view. Throughout SOF, the Habits of Mind form our main instructional framework. Writing, research and critical thinking skills, and exhibition-like projects are scaffolded for students from grades 6 to 12.

The Habits of Mind at the School of the Future Reflect Five of the Categories of the Exhibition Rubric

Point of View

From what point of view are we looking at this topic? Student should be able to identify the existing point of view of research and/or clearly establish from what lens he or she is approaching a given topic. This habit of mind is used to establish an argument.

Evidence

What is the evidence used to support the major point of view, argument, or hypothesis? Student should be able to find, digest, and analyze material

(Continued)

relevant to the chosen topic and be able to integrate the evidence so that it supports the thesis of the paper. Sources of evidence should come from a wide variety of media including but not limited to texts, reference books, periodicals, video clips, interviews, online periodicals, and vetted Internet sites. The Internet should not be the only source for an exhibition paper.

Connections

What are the connections of content within the chosen topic? How is the chosen topic connected to other content areas covered in and/or outside of class? This habit of mind asks the student to dig deep into his or her topic to find connections between content areas under investigation, between the relevance of content and self as learner, and to similar areas of study that are related to, but not explicitly part of the chosen topic.

Alternatives (Opposing Viewpoints/Supposition)

After thoroughly investigating a topic, alternatives to the original point of view must be explored. What other point of view can be used to investigate this topic? How would the outcome be affected if a variable were changed? The student is expected to explore theories or counterarguments that challenge the argument set forth in the paper or that in some way would alter the outcome (math/science).

Significance

Why is the topic under investigation important to the student and within the larger context of society? What difference or what impact does this topic have on a grand scale? This habit of mind is meant to get the student to think about and identify applications of the chosen topic outside of the classroom, to branch out and apply his or her knowledge to the commonality of daily life, or to demonstrate an understanding of the implications of the topic to society.

Communication

Although not part of the Habits of Mind, communication is part of the grading rubrics. Using the Habits of Mind as tools for exploration is key to developing a well-rounded exhibition paper. Being able to communicate findings, arguments, and counterarguments is likewise a key component of the paper. Using standard grammatical rules of formal writing, as well as quotes, diagrams, graphs, charts, and pictures when necessary, is essential to communicating thoughts and ideas.

In addition, exhibitions embody many of the CES Common Principles (listed in Chapter Two and online at www.essentialschools.org): using one's mind well; less is more; goals apply to all students; personalization; student as worker/teacher as coach; and demonstration of mastery.

These principles are all evident throughout the exhibition process from the student-sponsor relationship to the final presentation highlighting the mastery of the topic. The final exhibition presentation reflects the Coalition principle of demonstration of mastery. A committee of one teacher facilitator, the sponsor, two students, and an adult from outside the school staff assesses the written exhibition based on the Habits of Mind. The participants read the paper before the presentation time. They meet first and decide whether the paper meets the standard to be able to present. The rubric is out of 24 and a paper must obtain a 15 to be able to present. If a student does not reach the 15 points needed to present, he or she is given feedback and continues to work with the sponsor until the next round.

The committee must be within two points of each other. If the committee is not in agreement then the facilitator leads a conversation using the rubric to move the score within 2 points. For example, if a committee member has given a mastery of distinction on "use of evidence" and the other committee members have lower scores, they will look at the paper and discuss that one category and decide whether the use of evidence was really outstanding (Mastery with Distinction) or adequate (Mastery). This is done for every category until there is agreement. Occasionally there is a committee that is deadlocked and the committee is cancelled and another committee is set up on a future day.

The reader reliability of the committee is important for the process. The final grade is reflecting the student's mastery of the topic; inflated grades would be as bad as scrubbing regents exams. This alternative assessment is a replacement for the state regent exams and must be graded even more rigorously if we are to maintain the waiver and truly prepare students for college. After the presentation the student is offered feedback on both the written paper and the presentation. We expect students to reflect and grow from this experience for their future academic work. The committee must be in agreement to protect the integrity of the process. Any inflation in grading may lead a student to get a higher score than really reflects the student's understanding of the subject area.

As a CES school we are always talking to students and involving them in our decision making. It only makes sense to have students involved in the grading of the process that they are required to pass to graduate. The student voice on the committee is very powerful. Since they are actually in the classes that the student is presenting about, they are able to ask very insightful questions. It is interesting that sometimes the students are tougher on student's work than the teachers are.

After the written paper is graded, the student is told whether he or she has scored sufficiently to present. The presentation is roughly 20 minutes, followed by a 10 minute question and answer period. The expectation of the presentation is to add to the paper with visuals, which may be movie clips, diagrams, manipulatives that show the historical context, literary concepts, or the math or science behind the exhibition. The question and answer period is marked by deeper critical thinking questions that may double check the presenter's understanding of the historical background, alternative points of view, or the relationship between the various variables in math or science. The questions push the student's thinking and allow the committee to determine whether he or she has mastered the material.

Students must do two humanities exhibitions to graduate. They can choose between historical research, literary criticism, original work, or foreign language to fulfill the requirement. The rubrics for these exhibitions have been developed along with the New York State Consortium Performance Standards rubrics over the past ten years. They go through constant update as we try to better prepare our students for college-level work.

The use of the Habits of Mind ensures students think deeply and critically about the specific essential question that they want to explore. They are not trying to cover all of global history or the field of chemistry in one portfolio. Students chose a topic about which they are passionate and the sponsor personalizes their support at the students' skill level. The exhibition paper and presentation allows students to demonstrate their mastery in each subject area.

Types of Rubrics

Each rubric represents a different kind of exhibition that a student can do. All of them fall within the three categories: humanities, math, or science. Note, the Foreign Language rubrics fall under humanities and can be viewed through either a literary or historical lens. Here is a list and brief description of the rubrics currently available.

Humanities

Historical Research

In this type of exhibition students take some historically significant topic or issue dealt with in class and investigate it further. Students are expected to take a debatable position on the issue, demonstrate knowledge of historical background information and the impact on present or future events, and apply the Habits of Mind.

Literary Criticism

In this type of exhibition students compare two or more works by academically recognized authors. Students investigate literary techniques, tools, and styles of the authors that form the basis of the thesis. Students are also expected to research and integrate established critiques of their chosen works when possible. Students make historical or contemporary connections to societal issues stemming from their chosen works, as well as apply all other habits of mind.

Original Work

In this type of exhibition students create their own work(s) such as short stories or poetry. These works are then compared to academically recognized authors/artists in the same genre; students discuss the specific influences and comparisons between their own work and those of the selected authors/artists. Students are expected to research existing criticisms of their chosen established artists. All habits of mind are applied in the process.

(Continued)

Foreign Language

In this type of exhibition students discuss the influence of different cultures on one another, incorporating historical dates and evidence used to make cultural comparisons. The demonstration and use of the target language is a large component of this exhibition. All habits of mind are applied in the process.

Science/Math

Math/Science Investigation/Experiment

In this type of exhibition students take a content topic studied in class and investigate its use in or appropriateness to specific applications outside of the classroom. Or students can design and conduct an experiment to collect and analyze data that will be used to support their hypothesis for a chosen topic. All habits of mind are applied in the process.

At SOF, we are committed to helping our students become critical thinkers and concerned citizens who are able to make sense of the world around them. In the exhibition, a contentious viewpoint that a student proves through evidence and examining the alternative points of view illustrates the critical thinking skills we emphasize in our teaching. Active minds make connections to other things they have learned, and we want our students to understand the relevance of what they are studying and develop their own interests to pursue. As Lisa Karlich, the senior physics teacher, explains, "The most powerful moment for me as an educator is when I see the pride, confidence, and sense of accomplishment in my students' eyes when they are presenting their exhibition after becoming masters of their topics. When they teach their committee something new, something they are passionate about, the exhibition process is truly a wonderful experience."

Here are some examples of exhibitions that show the type of thinking we are striving for: Does human nature allow Communism to be successful? How can we use quadratic equations to find the height of falling objects? How does understanding Newton's Laws lead to improved safety features in automobiles? What is the symbolic significance of ghosts in Amy Tan's novels?

The exhibition process allows students to use their academic skills to develop an intellectual curiosity about topics of their choice. When students return from college the one thing they credit with their success is their involvement in the exhibition process. As a current junior recently told me, "The exhibition process veers away from the boring, tedious, traditional way of learning and incorporates both skills and information that we learn in the classroom with skills and information that we discover and research on our own. Exhibitions teach us one of the most imperative and fundamental skills necessary to survive in this world: persuasively defending a point of view through through evidence and in-depth analysis. Exhibitions are a way of taking what we learn in class and seeing how it pertains to life outside of school—or as many kids call it "the real world."

Our graduation rates are much higher than the city average, and we are tracking our students in college to ensure they are graduating from college and if not, why are they not graduating. Our guiding question is always, What can we do while they are at SOF to ensure their success?

Students as Workers, Teachers as Coaches

The teachers at SOF work very hard. They know they are working in a dynamic environment, where they are allowed a lot of freedom to develop their own curricula and be creative in their goals for the students. The students also realize they are in a different type of school and they are very proud of it. A 2005 graduate wrote, "SOF has allowed me to be a part of an environment where I am supported to explore myself as a learner and to learn how to think." As part of the CES Small Schools Network we have been able to take teachers and students to meetings throughout the year to represent the school and learn best practices at other schools. This adds to a buzz of excitement of what we are trying to accomplish at the School of the Future. In the CES *Essential Visions* video series, SOF was selected for the first DVD documenting "student as worker, teacher as coach." This honor has helped us document our instruction and strengthen the conversation within the school. The parents' commitment has been invaluable in our growth as a school. Parent Beth Bernett said this of her son's experience: "He enthusiastically researched his topics, using a variety of sources, to write papers that utilized critical thinking about his topics while satisfying demanding rubrics. Adding another layer of learning and accomplishment, using his creativity, he was able to communicate and demonstrate his mastery of these topics in multimedia presentations to panels of peers and adults that were as compelling to observe as they were for him to prepare." At SOF we also have Exhibition Teach-Ins where parents and local VIPs are invited to attend exhibition presentations, thus extending our outreach to parents and the community.

Lessons Learned

The exhibition process at the SOF is far from perfect. We are constantly striving to make the process better. A student recently told me, "One of the negative aspects of the exhibition process is that instead of viewing it as an exciting way to exhibit what they learned in school, some students view it as just a necessary component to graduate. But it is more valuable to those students than doing the regents exams." Often students do not realize the value until they go off to college. At SOF Alumni days, the majority of students comment on how much the exhibition process helped them be successful in college. Lisa Karlich notes that "it is difficult to manage such a large group of individual projects well on a consistent basis. Consequently, the exhibition process can lose its power and excitement when it is looked at as merely a perfunctory chore either by students or staff."

Creating intellectual curiosity and developing academically and socially responsible students will always be our focus. One hundred percent of our students go to college. Our success will be measured by their success in the real world. We will continue to fight to maintain our waiver from the regent exams. Alternative assessment will always have a place at SOF.

Reflection Questions

1. How do you assess your students? Is there a common practice used? How effective is your current practice?

2. Do any kinds of personalized assessments already occur in your school? How can you build on things you are already doing?

3. How can exhibitions be used in your school to augment the high-stakes assessments used in many states to create a better method of determining what a student knows and is able to do?

4. What kind of staff development is necessary to support student exhibitions? What kind of supports will students need in order to become proficient at exhibitions?

Resources

Coalition of Essential Schools, www.essentialschools.org

Davidson, J. (2007). Exhibitions: Demonstrations of mastery in essential schools. *Horace, 23.* www.essentialschools.org/resources/237.

DiMartino, J. (2007). Accountability or mastery? *Education Week, 26*(34).

DiMartino J., & Castaneda, A. (2007). Assessing applied skills. *Educational Leadership Magazine.*

DiMartino, J., Castaneda, A., Brownstein, M., & Miles, S. (2007). Authentic assessment. *Principal's Research Review, 2*(4).

DiMartino, J., & Clarke, J. (2008). *Personalizing the High School Experience for Each Student.* Alexandria, VA: ASCD.

DiMartino, J., Mangiante, E., & Miles, S. (2006). *High Schools at Work: Creating Student-Centered Learning* (DVDs with facilitator's guide). Alexandria, VA: ASCD.

New York State Performance Standards Consortium, http://performanceassessment.org

PART THREE Sowing the Seeds for Change

Collaborative Leadership

Changes and Challenges to the Idea of "Traditional" Neighborhood Schools

Virginia Eves

Madison High School, San Diego, California

Who would have thought that accepting the position of principal at Madison High would result in many sleepless nights (I suspect not too unusual for most principals), student walk-outs (also, while uncommon, not unprecedented), and repeated public comparisons to the "Grinch Who Stole Christmas" (quite unusual, I am told)? Although these events were hurtful and heartbreaking to me, nothing compared to the most frightening all—a dead rat arriving at my home by mail accompanied by a death threat, and another letter with a death threat containing a "suspicious" substance arriving at school. Most school leaders know that students occasionally do things of this nature, but at Madison High, many of these events appeared to have been orchestrated by adults from the school.

This assignment was certainly my most challenging in terms of leadership and work, but also in terms of examining my own personal beliefs about people. Because of my education and training as a counselor and family therapist, I have always been optimistic about human nature and believed in the goodness of mankind. But this position challenged me to rethink all that I had come to accept as fundamental to my belief system.

How It Began

In July 1999, I applied for a principal's position in San Diego Unified School District (SDUSD). New district leadership had resulted in three vacant positions for high school principal at both comprehensive and continuation sites. I was excited and anxious for the opportunity to take on the challenges of my first principalship after having worked at the district office for the previous four years. My expectation was the same as many others: that the interim principals (previously sitting vice principals at the two comprehensive sites) would get the principal positions, as they knew the students, staff, and community and had worked at the schools for several years. To my surprise (and the surprise of others) I was appointed principal of Madison High.

Even though the school had earned a bad reputation over the past several years, I believed that with focused effort on improvement from the students, staff, parents, and community, we could improve the reputation and give the community a school of which to be proud. The Academic Performance Index improvement target score was only for a gain of ten points, which I thought we could achieve without a tremendous amount of effort—just focused instruction and a will to improve from students and staff. I had worked with the staff and administration at the school a few times in the past, and although I didn't know them very well, I felt prepared and comfortable that my past experiences as teacher, counselor, head counselor, vice principal, and professional development administrator would serve me well as I assumed the role of principal. My attitude was optimistic, upbeat, excited, and filled with anticipation for the coming year.

My excitement with my new job lasted for less than one-half hour! From the very beginning I was confronted by many resistant staff members who made it clear they did not want me there; they wanted the former principal back and if not him, then the current vice principal whom they had known for more than five years. Discomfort, both theirs and mine, was everywhere. Conversations were difficult and strained, information was withheld, and obstacles were put in my way. Although no one openly attacked me on that first day, it became abundantly clear that I was not going to be supported by most of the current staff members. Fortunately, good times were ahead—very, very far ahead! Ultimately, we were able to overcome much adversity for the good of the students and the school community.

Getting to Work

Because I had never been a principal before and I realized I would receive little or no assistance from many of the staff, I decided to spend my first few weeks listening to students, attending all school events, and scheduling one-on-one time with each of the staff. I began by meeting after school with departments, where staff members could feel there was safety in numbers for them. My questions were simple and brief, and at the end of the meetings I scheduled one-on-one time with each department member during their preparation periods to further our conversations. By the end of the sixth week of school, I had met with nearly every staff member, certificated and classified. I had attended almost 30 school activities and community meetings—from sporting events (including football and volleyball games, track meets, and tennis matches) to PTA, Foundation, and Town Council meetings. In addition, I met with student clubs and their sponsors, athletic teams and their coaches, and the student leadership group. I greeted students every day as they arrived at school with their parents or on the school bus, and I also talked with them informally on the lunch court. I encouraged students, staff, parents, and community members to come see me if they had personal or confidential matters to discuss. My calendar became jam-packed, but the time was well spent.

In addition to gathering every conceivable type of verbal input about the school, I researched documents, test scores, and the past history of the school, trying to find good news that had occurred there in the past. Unfortunately, there was little good news to find in the last several years.

The History

I learned from several sources that during a teachers' strike in February 1995 Madison High School became the "go to" school for the media. The teachers' union members at the school, known as a union stronghold, were successful in preventing all but one teacher from crossing the picket line, at times by using forceful tactics. The strike lasted for five days and Madison High gained much notoriety during that time. This helped me understand why, on my first day with the full staff in 1999, I was confronted by a majority of the teachers wearing their "I held the line" T-shirts from the 1995 teachers' strike. During this same meeting, one of the teachers stood in the back of the room and announced that the previous principal "had died for their sins," and he was not going to stop protesting until the district answered his questions as to why.

Madison High School was labeled an underperforming high school by the district in Spring 1997, and was the only one receiving the designation located in a part of the city that had traditionally been known for its high-performing high schools. In fact Madison High had at one time been one of the academic and athletic powerhouses in the entire city for many years. As a result, Madison was named as a high school that must undergo the Process for Accountability Review (PAR); one of the issues was that grades were going up while test scores were going down.

The first part of the PAR process resulted in a team of district employees—teachers, principals, and central office managers—spending several days at the school investigating what might be done to improve student achievement, a process not unlike an accreditation visit. The school then had to write an extensive action plan that addressed the needs that were found and to determine what to do about improving student achievement. The perception by many staff and community members at the time was that the district was "out to get them," and it was using inappropriate data to single out certain schools, including Madison.

In Spring 1998 an undercover drug sting was put in place by the San Diego Police Department and SDUSD that resulted in the arrest of several students for dealing drugs on campus. The undercover operation was not a unique situation for SDUSD, but the timing for Madison High was unfortunate, as it followed closely on the heels of the recent PAR process and lent credence to the community perception of Madison High not only as an underperforming school, but also now as a "druggie" school. The community began to believe that students needed to go to a different neighborhood school to be in a drug-free environment.

Adding to the unsavory reputation of the school was its appearance. Madison High became the "poster child" for how rundown a school could become. The newly appointed superintendent held the kick-off press conference for a $1.51 billion dollar school bond issue at Madison because the media could show neglected, ugly, broken, disintegrating buildings, mold, dangerous walkways, leaky roofs, exterior stucco peeling and discolored, as well as interior classrooms that were in a state of disrepair. In the accreditation report done the next year, the visiting committee noted the rundown and neglected state of the school. It was not a welcoming place.

The 1998–1999 school year was the most tragic year of all. A special education teacher was arrested on campus and accused of having a loaded gun in his possession, which he had carried for a number of months in the presence of students who were severely disabled both mentally and physically. His students participated in community-based instruction (CBI), which required him to transport students in his car. He was accused of carrying the gun to and from the classroom, and having it in the classroom and in his car in the presence of students—another severe and highly public blow to the reputation of the school.

Later in that same year, the head football coach of seven years was arrested and accused of soliciting underage boys for inappropriate purposes. His trial resulted in his conviction and his sentencing to several years of incarceration. It is no surprise that by now what had been a community perception of an unsavory atmosphere at Madison High was coupled with serious safety concerns for the children—many of which were caused by the adult staff on the campus, not students or outsiders. As a result, parents in large numbers were pursuing other options for their children to attend high school.

In June 1999 the well-loved principal of seven years was re-assigned to the classroom amid much public controversy, media coverage, and staff and parent consternation. While I was aware of these last two major and public "black eyes" for the school, I did not realize how terribly the school's reputation had eroded in the community over the past several years.

More Bad News

Within the first month of my assignment to the school, a 16-year-old sophomore was arrested with a loaded gun on campus. The gun was tied to a homicide, and the student is now serving a life sentence for murder. More negative press for the school. More reasons for parents to send their students to other schools.

The Disconnect

As I finished meeting with the staff during the first few weeks of the school year, I was continually struck by the huge disconnect between what the facts told me and what many of the staff believed about the school. These staff members truly and consistently believed themselves to be victims of a plot by the district to publicly embarrass them and to single them out and make an example of Madison High. They denied that the school was underperforming; they denied that there were good reasons for parents not to send their kids to the school; they denied that the test scores truly reflected a school in trouble; and they denied that there were any concerns about instructional practices or grades at the school.

Many of those same staff members claimed that the major reason Madison had such a bad reputation was that the Voluntary Ethnic Enrollment Program or VEEP buses for integration had arrived, and "those" kids would never achieve at high levels. Their perception was that the neighborhood had changed and that the current students were kids of blue collar workers who could not be expected to achieve at the high levels of the students who had come before when the neighborhood had families of higher socioeconomic level. "If the district would just leave us alone and let us teach these students skills they need for service jobs and not for college, we could become a vocational school focused on the trades." This was typical of statements made at PTA meetings, staff meetings, in one-on-one meetings, and in the community.

The Changing Face of Madison High

Students. When I arrived in 1999, Madison's school community consisted of approximately 1,500 students: 43 percent free and reduced lunch; 30 percent English language learners (ELL); 15 percent students with special needs; 23 percent VEEP students transported on buses from other parts of the city; 24 percent Gifted and Talented education students; and a 42 percent college-going rate. As a result, Madison High's distribution of ethnicity almost perfectly matched the diversity of the City of San Diego at large.

Staff. The staff consisted of about 120 staff members with an average age of 50+ and very little ethnic diversity. Only one person in the administrative offices spoke Spanish, yet some 30% of the students were ELL, and their parents were primarily Spanish speakers. Only about 20% of the faculty held a Crosscultural Language and Academic Development (CLAD) or equivalent certificate although the state mandated it for all teachers in 1991.

Parents. The surrounding resident community of Madison High had changed over time from one of white- and blue-collar upwardly mobile Caucasian workers to one of predominantly blue-collar ethnically diverse workers. As a result, some of the local resident community's perception was inconsistent with the data; many of the active Caucasian residents believed that the students who arrived on the VEEP buses were the majority of the school population and wholly responsible for the academic decline of the school. There was little desire to understand that the demographics of the entire community had changed, and that only one-fourth of the students arrived on the integration buses. Adding to the misperceptions about the school was the fact that many of the Caucasian parents had also graduated from Madison during a demographically different generation.

First Steps

During the one-on-one confidential meetings with students, staff, and parents, I was very clear about what I needed to know. I always asked the same simple questions:

1. What, if anything, needs to change?
2. What should *not* change?

What to Change?

Making decisions about what to change, and in what order, required me to gather information from a variety of sources. I met with students, staff members, parents, and community members to get their ideas about what their needs and priorities were.

Students' Input

Two high-achieving seniors from the Class of 2000 wanted a confidential meeting with me to discuss the curriculum and safety at our school. They wanted me to know that the teachers didn't treat kids fairly, in their opinion, and that the teachers didn't think Madison students could do rigorous college preparatory work. They went on to give me example after example of how misbehaving students weren't held accountable for their actions and as a result they often felt unsafe on campus. They also told me that teachers seemed to "pick on" certain students, especially if the students rode the VEEP buses. They reported that many teachers were frustrated with student misconduct and that they often aired their frustrations in their classes.

According to the students, teachers believed that they should simply prepare students to go to work after high school, because they were not "college-going" material. They wanted me to know that while some students might need a bit more help than in some of the other schools, they were very smart and capable of taking hard classes and they *wanted* to go to college. These two students believed that the school had let them down because they could not compete on the college entrance applications with students from neighboring schools. They pointed out that our school only offered four AP courses while other high schools offered 15 to 20. They wanted me to know that although it was too late for them, they wanted to help the students in the coming years. They wanted future students to be competitive on their transcripts and to be able to vie for slots at the most prestigious universities in the country. It saddened them that the teachers did not believe in them. They asked that I do everything in my power to convince the staff that "really smart kids went to our school."

After meeting with those senior students, I talked with many other students who shared similar stories. Students felt disadvantaged because, in their opinion, their teachers and counselors had done little to help them prepare for rigorous college course work, did little to assist them with completing college applications, and did little to help them apply for college financial aid, which they knew they would desperately need. Stories of this nature came from all quarters of the student population; yet teachers and counselors believed they were doing everything in their power to assist kids; it was just that these kids weren't college material—they needed to go to work. The following list summarizes the requests for change from students. The items were quite simple to state, but quite another thing to accomplish. Their list included

- Make the school safe
- Hire more teachers and counselors who care about us
- Create a school we can be proud of
- Offer more advanced, Advanced Placement, and Advancement Via Individual Determination (AVID) classes
- Make sure our counselors know about college entrance requirements and financial aid

Teacher and Staff Input

Input from teachers and staff was surprisingly similar to the students' except for the disconnect that I mentioned earlier—their perception that the students had changed and couldn't be expected to reach high standards because they had too many obstacles to overcome. The school needed to be a vocational school, so the students could learn to work with their hands because they just weren't college material. Teachers' and staff input for change included

- Make the school safe
- Create a school we can be proud of
- Remove the "underperforming" label because it was not justified
- Become a vocational/trade school to reflect the community change from white collar to blue collar

Parents' and Community Input

The parents' and community list was quite similar to that of the students, teachers, and staff. Their list included

- Make the school safe
- Create a school we can be proud of "like it used to be"
- "Become a vocational/trade school because, in this community, the kids [except their own, who needed the advanced courses] need to learn to work with their hands. Service jobs are important to our economy." (from a PTSA Parent)

I found it sad that so many people expected so little of the current students.

What Not to Change?

In my discussions with the various consitutuencies about what needed to change, I also learned about things that were important to students, staff, parents, and community members that should be included in the new school design.

Students' Input

The list from the students was quite short:

- Drama
- Chorus
- AJROTC

Other than these three things about the school that had good student support and appreciation, there was little else that the students thought didn't need fixing—the teachers, the counselors, the coaches, and even the custodians. The students also stated the obvious: that the facilities were ugly and run down and in dire need of a massive facelift.

Teachers' and Staff Input

The teachers and staff had quite a different perspective on what they felt should not be changed. Their list was long and seemed to focus entirely on the needs and wishes of adults. They wanted to "keep the fun." When asked what that meant, they listed such things as

- Keep frequent Happy Hour gatherings at the local tavern
- Keep all-day Friday potluck events that were held all day every Friday in the Principal's Conference Room

Although I believe social activities are important to a school culture, what I found shocking was that faculty and staff would often come to school events after the Happy Hour gatherings under the influence and sometimes even in supervisory capacities. When I made it clear that supervisors could not work if they had been drinking, and as staff accountability for various site policies and procedures were enforced, I was accused of being the "Grinch Who Stole Christmas." In addition, when I suggested that the Friday potluck event be moved to the Staff Lounge because it was more centrally located and because the Principal's Conference Room was often needed for student, staff, and parent conferencing, the staff felt that I had "robbed" them of their opportunity for social interaction—no one wanted to go the Staff Lounge because treats were better in the "office." The faculty and staff did, however, agree with the students on some additional things that should not be changed:

- Keep the visual and performing arts program, particularly drama and chorus
- Keep the AJROTC program

Parents' and Community Input

The parents had a short list, just like the students. The only things they felt were worth saving included

- Drama
- Chorus
- AJROTC

The Challenge Defined

My tasks, although quite short in number, seemed daunting to approach. I only needed to make the school safe, dramatically improve student achievement, find teachers and counselors who cared more about students, improve all the extra-curricular activities except drama, chorus, and AJROTC, and, oh yes, oversee the implementation of Proposition MM (the $1.5 billion facilities-improvement bond initiative) that would result in over $8 million of improved facilities and learning environments for the students of Madison High. All of this had to be accomplished, of course, in a mere four years! Hardly a challenge at all!

Redesigning a Belief System

My belief system is based on my own story, as well as my work with students as a teacher, counselor, and administrator, and is aligned with those of researchers such as Katie Haycock, Richard Elmore, and Linda Darling-Hammond, the National Center on Education and the Economy, as well as many others.

I believe that students will accomplish whatever we expect of them, and that the challenge for the adults is to convince students that they can accomplish whatever they set their minds to—*conceive, believe, achieve.* I also believe that students need to have personal connections to school outside the classroom; they need to be in activities where they can be more involved and committed to personal growth and achievement. Students can get to know a mentor and have the opportunity to receive guidance from a significant adult in their lives, someone other than their parents. Students can start to create their futures.

I also believe that in spite of difficult parents or home conditions, students will achieve for teachers who care deeply about their students; that students will overcome great adversity if they know their teachers expect them to meet high standards and will provide support for them to reach those standards. The research is clear that students suffer greatly from continued exposure to average or less than average teachers, but that they progress tremendously when they have teachers who use powerful teaching strategies and provide support, especially for those students who have been traditionally underserved.

Conceive

By November of that first year, I had a clear vision of what needed to be accomplished. The priorities were also clear. We had to first make the campus safe.

Second, we had to tackle the very difficult work of improving student achievement. And finally, we had to integrate facilities improvement work with both safety and improved teaching and learning.

The Renaissance of Madison High

My vision for the school was dubbed by a friend as, "The Renaissance of Madison High." I wanted the school to be able to return to its former glory both academically and in extracurricular activities; I wanted the school to have a fair, firm, and consistent Student Management (discipline) Plan; I wanted all students to be prepared to pursue any postsecondary plan that would lead them to the standard of living to which we all aspire—"gold collar" jobs; and I wanted no student to be thought of as a future "blue collar worker" or to be prevented from pursuing what we have formerly referred to as "white collar jobs." If all students graduated from Madison High with the knowledge and skills necessary for lifelong learning as stated in our mission, then every child would have the opportunity to become whatever she or he wanted to be by pursuing an education to whatever level desired.

The founder of AVID, Mary Catherine Swanson, has stated that "Rigor without support is an unrealistic expectation, and support without rigor is wasted potential." That quote perfectly describes how I felt about Madison High students based on my many conversations with them.

So, how would this Renaissance look? Every student would graduate with 15–25 college units; every student would meet college entrance requirements by the end of their senior year; every student would have the opportunity to take AP and rigorous college preparatory courses; every student would have academic support through literacy and math support classes, AVID, after-school tutoring, and student support groups; every student would participate in at least one school club, sport, or school activity; every student would have a postsecondary plan prepared during their sophomore year; every student would have the opportunity to explore the career world and have the opportunity for adult work immersion via job shadows, internships, and exploratory work experience; most important, every student would be taught and counseled by the very best teachers and counselors we could find. If we could accomplish all of this, then the school would truly be able to return to its former glory! The questions, of course, were, Could we really make all of this happen, and how could I find the right people to help?

I could *not* reconcile the seeming disconnect between teachers firmly believing that the school was doing the best it could given the student population, and what I believed to be true about setting high standards for students. Research is rich with evidence that supports the importance of setting high standards, and there are many success stories of schools that have been very successful with students who "looked" just like ours! No matter how often we discussed research of this nature in staff meetings there was very little change in the staff's perception that they could not teach our students to perform at high levels. As our leadership team discussed this dilemma toward the end of my first year, we came to realize that perhaps the issue was more about teachers believing in themselves. We needed to change their beliefs about themselves and their influence on students before we could expect them to change their beliefs about our students.

Putting first things first, during the first few months of that first year, it was clear that safety was on everyone's mind. I often worried about what I saw happening on campus and in classrooms. Teachers weren't feeling supported by the counselors and the administrators; students weren't feeling safe on the lunch court and between classes. Clearly, we had to solve that issue before we could tackle belief systems.

Safety First

The majority of that first year was spent with students, staff (certificated and classified), administration, and parents meeting to research and design a student management system that would keep everyone safe, allow teachers to teach, and assure parents that their children would be safe at school. The plan needed to be fair, firm, and consistent, easily understood by all, clearly enforced, and frequently communicated to all constituents. This was an onerous but necessary task; the plan we developed was a composite of plans from other schools, clearly and simply written to address the needs of our students, staff, and parents. I decided that we should implement the plan before the end of the school year so that we could work out any "bugs" before the opening of the next school year. It seemed like a good idea at the time, and looking back now, it was a good idea. However, on May 1, 2000, a student walk-out occurred in protest of the new plan.

Given the recent history at Madison High, local media was immediately on site and police cars were in large supply. Only later did I find out that some of our own staff members had helped to organize the students, phoned the media, and given students tips on how to most effectively stage a walk-out. To their credit, the walk-out was quite effective, but we did not change the rules, and by the end of the year, students and staff had come to accept that the rules were there to stay and in fact, students, staff, and parents started to comment that it seemed like the plan was working. At long last we were seeing our first success story!

Another surprise to me was the need to regularly discipline adults for inappropriate behaviors. Unfortunately, there were several other incidents involving adults on campus that continued to keep Madison in a negative spotlight. Most of the adult misbehavior did not make the headlines, but we had some very close calls. Fortunately, with the arrival of a very good school police officer, we were able to be proactive and prevent "headline news" by getting to the problem on the first report of misconduct. Because students were feeling safer on campus, and because we were doing assemblies about both student *and* adult behavior, students began to feel comfortable reporting inappropriate behaviors, not just by students, but also by staff. During my first three years, many reports from students about individual staff members were investigated with appropriate disciplinary actions taken when necessary.

By the start of my third year at Madison, student (and staff) behaviors improved dramatically. Our crime reports were greatly reduced, and our safe campus statistics greatly improved; we had become one of the safest campuses in the district.

Believe

Although Madison High had already been named an underperforming school by the district in 1997, it was during my first day on the job in 1999 that the State of California named Madison High an underperforming school. However, because it was my first day, the school was allowed a year's reprieve. At the start of my second year, we now had to address this new state label of underperforming. While no one welcomes that designation, there were good things about how the state implemented the Immediate Intervention/Underperforming Schools Program (II/USP) Grant, a three-year grant that Madison received to plan and implement strategies that would result in improved student achievement. Year One, the planning year, was spent with an outside consultant who worked with the staff to determine what we could do to improve student achievement. The II/USP plan designed by the staff requested an attendance coordinator, common planning time, lower class size, professional development and training in literacy and math strategies, additional support materials, curriculum writing time in the summer, and additional support for struggling readers and writers. District initiatives had also determined that all students below grade level would have extended time in literacy and math, resulting in block classes.

In Years Two and Three, the State gave significant additional monies to fund all the items that had been requested by the staff. This was a wonderful boost to staff morale and it resulted in additional support for students. For once, we could afford the strategies and supplies that the staff believed would help to improve student achievement.

In spite of this good news, however, we continued to cope with an undercurrent of some of the staff and their belief that we could not expect great things from students like ours. Even with additional funding and a "grassroots" plan, some staff still perceived our students as "not able"—not in an unkind way, but in a sympathetic way. We also had our accreditation midterm visit which brought new information about Madison High. When the Visiting Committee arrived in 2002 and reviewed our midterm report, they shared that the previous six-year term of accreditation had not come without much controversy among the members of the 1999 Visiting Committee. Although the committee found the 1999 Accreditation Report helpful, and believed that the Action Plan designed by the school would bring about necessary changes, the Visiting Committee also added eight areas of need the school had to address before the midterm visit in 2002. When the committee shared the exit report with the staff in 1999 before I arrived at the school, the committee was appalled by the disrespectful treatment they received from the staff and the argumentative accusations made by the staff toward the Visiting Committee. The staff had openly and aggressively accused the Visiting Committee of including inaccuracies and untrue items in the report. The committee members were so upset by these accusations that they considered withdrawing their recommendation for a six-year term of accreditation with a midterm visit, and recommending only a one-year term because the committee members were afraid the staff did not take their report seriously and would not make any attempt to make the changes the report required. They finally decided to give a six-year term with a midterm visit after much discussion and the expectation that the school would do what was recommended in the report. This new information helped me understand more about behaviors I had observed among the some of the staff and gave more credence to the stories I had heard from students, parents, and even some other staff members.

The question remained, however, where do we go from here? What were we to do to accomplish the work set out in the accreditation Action Plan and get our staff to believe in our students?

Developing the Plan

I knew that I had to use every strategy available to secure the very best teachers and counselors for our students, the majority of whom would fit the description of underserved. Although the II/USP plan helped us with concrete parts of improving student achievement, we had to be more surreptitious in finding ways to change teachers' beliefs about our students. Some of the strategies we used to renew teachers' faith in themselves included:

- Focusing on activities that would renew their confidence in teaching
- Leading them to recognize how important they are in their students' lives
- Seeing what a difference they could make in their students' lives, just as teachers had in their own lives
- Acknowledging how much power they have in their students' lives—hearing it from the students
- Publicly validating and recognizing teachers' accomplishments
- Having recent graduates come back and tell teachers some of the discouraging words they had been told in our classrooms and counselors' offices
- Having focus groups of students and parents led by university consultants and reported to staff using actual words of the students and parents
- Surveying all students, parents, and staff members regarding campus safety, instructional practice, resources, rules, and so forth
- Forming a Student Advisory Group that met with me once a month to discuss campus concerns, complaints, and issues
- Holding faculty meetings focused on empowering teachers
- Showing motivational movies demonstrating how important teachers are in children's lives
- Sharing and discussing literature focused on successful schools and students that are similar to ours
- Displaying motivational posters throughout the school honoring teachers and teaching

Other factors also influenced our efforts in developing a stronger belief in our students. During my third year (2002–2003), the district offered a retirement incentive for veteran staff. As I mentioned earlier, the average age of the staff when I arrived was 50+. As in most high schools throughout the district, Madison High was significantly impacted by the attrition of veteran teachers. During that year, we hired 37 new teachers, nearly one third of the staff, as a result of the retirement incentive. In addition, because of the district's focus on block classes in literacy and math and the new focus on more AP and community college course offerings, GATE certification for teachers, and career path sequences with articulated community college courses, we hired an additional 23 teachers the following year. In fact, by the time of our six-year accreditation visit in 2004–2005, more than 90% of the staff were new to the school.

Improving Student Achievement Through Professional Development

Because the II/USP plan designed by staff called for much professional development and common planning time, we were able to use that time to address the disconnect I mentioned earlier. We needed to encourage our teachers to have faith in themselves, to renew their commitment to teaching and to students, to remember how important teachers had been in their lives, and to connect emotionally to the students in their classes. We used several strategies over time, so it is hard to know what worked and what didn't. I tend to believe it was the collective effect of all that we did that made the difference.

Some of the Strategies We Implemented with Our Faculty and Staff

- Inviting students to staff meetings three times per year to discuss powerful teaching and learning, teaching strategies that worked for them, and classroom environments that would support improved student achievement
- Requiring monthly professional development days for each core department focused on teaching to high standards, examining student work

(*Continued*)

and data, planning backward, and using common assessments and grading standards

- Encouraging all departments to meet monthly and focus on the same things as the core departments
- Offering summer planning time for all teachers
- Encouraging, supporting, and validating professional growth
- Encouraging teachers to share their learning with others
- Inviting students to faculty meetings to discuss what good teaching and learning looks and sounds like
- Designing syllabi and daily agendas with student input
- Designing user-friendly advisory curriculum with student input
- Beginning the Link Crew Program, which supported incoming grade nine students during the transition into high school
- Offering "Cocoa and Cram" sessions at the end of each semester to focus students on the importance of studying for final exams as they would in college
- Selecting essential standards that everyone agreed to work on to improve student skills regardless of content area
- Encouraging summer readings of books such as *Mosaic of Thought, Entertaining an Elephant, I Read and I Still Don't Get It, The Power of Their Ideas,* and *The Tipping Point*
- Reflecting on and discussing the summer readings in pre-school meetings to discover what we might use to help our students
- Listening to motivational speakers who could tell how other schools like ours overcame barriers and improved student achievement
- Establishing classroom learning environments with input from students to support student success and to welcome students to the classroom (print-rich, common daily agenda template: standards-driven lessons: homework assignments with "look ahead" reminders: classroom libraries)
- Surrounding teachers with literature-rich classroom libraries

- Holding faculty meetings focused on examining data and reviewing educational research literature
- Encouraging teachers to greet and welcome students with encouraging words every day as they entered the classroom, thus building self-confidence in the students
- Requiring every staff member to serve on an "I's Have It" Committee (Intervention, Instruction, Incentives) to develop strategies focused on improved student performance and increased student self-confidence

"I's Have It" Committees developed wonderful lesson plans, incentives, and interventions that taught, supported, and motivated students to care more, work harder, achieve more, participate in more school activities, and prepare for the exit exams and standardized testing.

The Changing Face of Madison High

Although improved student achievement through purposeful planning and strong professional development activities remained central to our work, we were concurrently undergoing a massive renewal of our facilities, both interior and exterior. Great disruption was created by ongoing construction, constant classroom relocations, and closure of the library resource center for over a year while a major expansion was completed.

Irrigation and electrical and heating systems were replaced; roofing was replaced throughout the entire campus; asbestos abatement procedures were undertaken in every classroom; lead paint removal occurred in all areas; high-speed fiber optic cable was installed throughout the campus; upgrades of all technology wiring and equipment were made: the Performing Arts Center was completely upgraded with the most advanced technology available; the gym ceiling and floor were entirely replaced; the softball field was relocated; all scoreboards were replaced; portable classrooms were recertified for earthquake safety; the Design and Technology Academy (one of our small learning communities) converted the old metal and wood shops into state-of-the-art engineering, robotics, and multi-media labs; the district's Gifted and Talented Education Department was relocated to our campus with four portable classrooms; and the

Deaf and Hard of Hearing (DHH) Regional Center, long located on Madison's campus, had to have special provisions made when their classrooms had to relocate for refurbishment.

This list could go on and on, but it is important to understand the magnitude of the challenges that students and staff overcame on our journey to making dramatic gains in student achievement. It was certainly a team effort and the students, staff, and parents deserve all the credit for keeping their eyes on the prize of improved student performance in spite of having every reason to give up and throw in the towel.

In addition to the many challenges caused by external disruptions to the learning environment on site, the statistical data and demographics of the school had changed dramatically as well. The chart below demonstrates the changes that had occurred in the student population.

Our Changing Face

Ethnic make-up*	1/3–1/3–1/3	→	1/2–1/4–1/4
Free and reduced lunch	43%	→	62%
English learners	30%	→	40%
Special education	15%	→	20%
(Bused integration)	23%	→	30%
Gifted and talented	24%	→	24%

* Hispanic, White, Other.

Achieve

The book *The Tipping Point* has greatly influenced my belief about our school, and I have come to look at Madison High's success as a series of "tipping points" that ultimately improved the culture, improved the community's perception, and increased the achievement of the students at the school. That is not to say that the school has achieved success, but I do believe it is much closer to regaining its former glory than it has been in the last 25 years.

Academic Focus

The focus we kept on student achievement was unwavering and is evidenced by the following:

- More than 70 hours of professional development per teacher per year on average
- Rigorous and relevant instruction focused on essential standards
- Curriculum development, pacing guides, common assessments, and grading standards in each core content area
- AVID implementation schoolwide with classroom and advisory lessons focused on AVID strategies
- Maintenance of literacy blocks with reduced class size for grades nine and ten even after the district mandate was discontinued
- Reduced counselor caseload
- Full-time psychologist
- Classroom libraries
- Enlarged and enhanced library resource center
- Exited the II/USP Program status as a result of improved student achievement
- Application for and receipt of additional external and grant funding
  - Small Learning Communities Grant
  - Perkins Grant
  - Data Facilitators' Grant
  - Striving Readers' Grant
  - Additional year of II/USP Grant funding because of Madison's dramatic improvement in student achievement
- Outsourcing of important projects and tasks to highly qualified retired administrators (e.g., master schedule, course catalogs, testing, social work and community support for families), thus saving tight budget dollars for student achievement work

Community Support—Other Signs of Success

National universities and foundations, as well as local community colleges and businesses, sought partnerships with Madison High. Partners included but were not limited to

- University of California, San Diego (UCSD)
- California State University, San Diego (SDSU)
- University of San Diego (USD)
- Point Loma Nazarene University
- Rochester Institute of Technology, Project Lead the Way Engineering Program, recognizes MHS Design and Technology Academy (DaTA)
- SDSU College of Engineering
- National University
- Alliant University
- San Diego Community College, Mesa Campus
- San Diego County Bar Association
- Job shadows
  - Peer Court
  - Legal Eagles—E-mentoring
  - Law Week
- National Aeronautics and Space Administration
- First Academy of Engineering (AOE) recognized by the National Academy Foundation
- FIRST/For Innovation in Science and Technology robotics competencies
- Grant Funding for Small Learning Communities—Design and Technology Academy, School of the Arts, AJROTC House, and the Frosh House using Link Crew strategies as its guiding principles
- Substantial financial support from alumni for students and programs in need
- Student participation in extracurricular activities increasing by over 300% with many championship awards given to teams, students, teachers, and coaches

Rewards and Recognition

Our journey was not unlike that of many other schools, and although challenging, arduous, and ongoing, the payoff for all of us is to see the gleam in students', staff's, and parents' eyes when they can once again be proud of the progress made.

Our Accomplishments

Here is a brief list of the most significant accomplishments that attest to the successful work of the students, staff, and parents:

- Received the maximum term of accreditation with accolades from every member of the Visiting Committee
- Named by *Newsweek* as one of America's Best High Schools for 2004–05, 2005–06, and 2006–07
- Exited accountability program for Immediate Intervention/Underperforming Schools Program
- Recognized by the American Youth Policy Forum for exemplary establishment of Small Learning Communities
- Named *2006 Breakthrough High School* by the Bill & Melinda Gates Foundation under the auspices of the National Association of Secondary School Principals; selection criteria included over 50% ethnic diversity; over 50% economically disadvantaged; and over 90% graduation rate; and over 90% postsecondary education rate

Lessons Learned

When I entered the environment of Madison High, which had resigned itself to the status quo and couldn't seem to gather the strength and momentum to overcome the inertia, I had to decide what I believed we could do and then try to figure out how to do it. I had to become the agent of change. It would have been much easier to appease the complacency; it was my obligation not to be complacent; the students, as our ambassadors to the future, desired and deserved the best I had to offer.

- To conceive: Determine where we needed to go.
- To believe: Gain the strength to do the work.
- To achieve: Enjoy the results of work well done.

When limitations evaporated and a future that was previously deemed impossible solidified before their eyes—I could see students, staff and parents accomplish things they never thought they could! Hope was re-awakened and revitalized—it was evident on their faces when their dreams became their realities. They were able to consider and create futures that they had once considered impossibilities.

I am proud of the progress we made at Madison High, but I know that the work must continue to focus on improving student achievement, making school more personal for students, and finding the very best teachers, counselors, and staff to support students who have been traditionally underserved. I feel most fortunate to have had the privilege to work with the students, staff, and parents of Madison High, for it is they who made the dreams of our students come true! I give my deepest heartfelt thanks to everyone who played such an important part in making the campus safe, in improving student achievement, and in improving the perception of our school in the community.

Reflection Questions

1. What is your problem situation? How do you as a school district or faculty describe it? What data have you used to define your problem?

2. How can the community be engaged to understand and support your school as changes to the traditional student demographics occur?

3. What stories do your students tell about the prominent events in their high school experience?

4. What kind of leadership is needed to support a climate of change in the school? What district support is necessary to support and sustain change in troubled schools? How can these support systems be sustained over time in order to give reforms an opportunity to take root and grow?

Resources

Breaking Ranks II: Strategies for Leading High School Reform. (2004). Alexandria, VA: NASSP.

Breaking Ranks: A Field Guide for Leading Change. (2008). Alexandria, VA: NASSP.

Brownstein, M., DiMartino, J., & Miles, S. (2007). Academic engagement of all students. *Principal's Research Review, 2*(3).

DiMartino, J., & Clarke, J. (2008). *Personalizing the High School Experience for Each Student.* Alexandria, VA: ASCD.

DiMartino, J., & Miles, S. (2006). Strategies for successful personalization. *Principal Leadership Magazine, 6*(10), 26–30.

DiMartino, J., & Miles, S. (2006). Leadership at school: How to get the job done. *Principal Leadership Magazine, 10,* 47–50.

DiMartino, J., & Wolk, D. (2004). Closing ranks: The evolution from *Breaking Ranks* to *Breaking Ranks II. The Vision Magazine, 3*(2), 23–26.

SERVE

Motivation: The Key to Success in Teaching and Learning Video Series: Motivationally Anchored Instruction, Motivationally Anchored Classrooms, and Motivationally Anchored Schools (2003). (DVDs with facilitator's guide). Alexandria, VA: ASCD.

Professional Learning Communities

Teachers Talking Together and the Power of Professional Community

Linda Nathan

Boston Arts Academy, Boston, Massachusetts

Boston Arts Academy (BAA) is part of the Boston Pilot Schools, a group of 20 innovative public schools within the Boston Public Schools (BPS) system. As a Pilot School, we have five distinct autonomies: curriculum, governance, staffing, scheduling and calendar, and budget. The pilots are similar to in-district charters, but we are within the system and charged with changing the system at the same time. It really is the best of all worlds. BAA was founded in 1998 and is the city's first and only high school for the visual and performing arts. It is in this environment of autonomy and innovation that we've been able to create opportunities for creating the kind of professional communities that makes teaching at BAA so special.

When we opened, I was determined to find veteran teachers to head the arts department, which we did, but because those jobs were going to be so hard I also wanted to recruit teachers who saw themselves as artist-scholars—the term we use to describe what we are creating with students, too. The founding teachers were people who had been trained at Fenway High School (another BPS Pilot School) or "Fenway-like" schools, or who wanted to be part of a new initiative or who believed in the arts as a way of transformation. That still holds true to this day. We try to have a mix of new teachers as well as veterans, and we do pretty well at striking that balance. We train a lot of our own new teachers through a program with Tufts University and other area universities. We also do teacher leadership training through the Principal Residency Network at Northeastern University. Whether we're recruiting new teachers or retaining our existing ones, being part of a professional community is a crucial element at BAA.

Demonstrating the Importance of Building Supportive Communities for Teachers

Last year we interviewed a prospective teacher, Jocelyn, for a science position. Jocelyn previously taught for a year in another urban school system and had used the same engineering curriculum we were implementing. We were excited that Jocelyn had worked as an engineer for a number of years, and that she was a young woman of color. But as the interview progressed, we were dismayed by the experiences she reported to us about her first year of teaching, experiences that unfortunately are all too common. In her school Jocelyn had taught more than 150 students a day, and although she benefited from a coach who visited her classroom every two weeks or so, no mentor teacher had been available to her. Her classes included a class labeled "behavioral students" even though she had only taken one summer school class in special education. She was supposed to have a special education teacher co-teach this behavior class with her, but this teacher was usually pulled out of class to keep up with the testing of special education students.

As we discussed her successes and challenges with the engineering curriculum, we learned that the resource kits had never arrived at her school and she was left to develop all the experiments herself from the textbook, and that she had spent literally thousands of dollars of her own money purchasing materials. We asked about professional development time and she looked at us quizzically. Does the faculty meet together to plan curriculum? Do faculty members observe one another teach? Jocelyn explained that as a member of the ninth grade team they had met together almost every day, but never to plan curriculum or talk about lessons; there wasn't time for that. The bulk of their meetings were spent discussing issues of attendance and tardiness, and submitting various forms to the district office so that the school would not lose money because of truancy. In addition, meeting time was filled with the all-consuming task of analyzing both quarterly citywide and annual state standardized tests in English, math, science, and history. Teachers would carefully analyze which items students did poorly on and map those back to the standards taught in order to figure out ways to "improve" their teaching. Although Jocelyn's students had not done well on the science test, they had done better than students in the other Boston high schools. Her administrator had congratulated her, but the scores for the rest of the district were abysmal. Jocelyn couldn't feel good about that. She told us, "There is just never time to talk about teaching since the analysis of test items is so time consuming." During the term, a literacy coach had met with the whole ninth grade team and reviewed strategies for incorporating literacy into all the content areas. Although Jocelyn found the ideas very interesting, she didn't feel that she was yet familiar enough with her own curriculum to think about an additional strand, and she worried that since no one ever observed her teaching literacy in her engineering curriculum that she wasn't doing a good job. "The goal was for all of us to teach a literacy block, but that never happened so we're just supposed to add it on to our primary content area. It's been a pretty overwhelming year. I guess I'm just looking for a school where I will get more support and where teachers actually talk about teaching instead of just test results and forms that have to be submitted to another office."

When I heard this committed, creative young teacher talk in ways that suggested she was burning out in a job she should have loved, what stood out to me was something that may not even be obvious to her. She was focused on herself: the demands on her individual time, the pressures of the job. What I heard was a story of the failure of a professional learning community.

On the surface, Jocelyn was doing what we ask all teachers to do: teach content in engaging ways to her students so that they could learn. This is, after all, what schools do: teach students. But that definition of school is at its most rudimentary. If schools are merely "content factories" (and I realize I'm exaggerating a bit here) they tend not to be professional learning communities. A professional learning community exists in a school when the entire faculty and staff, including the administration, works together toward a shared set of standards and assessments that are known to all in the school community. Usually, those standards and the assessments to measure whether students have met them are developed by the teachers in the school, or a close network of schools. Furthermore, such a school is a learning environment for all the adults. No one feels that they have "got it right" and that no more learning as a teacher is necessary. Standards and assessments are continually re-tooled as teachers and students become more proficient. A school that is also a professional learning community recognizes that the work with students and with the adults is ongoing and embodies the value of continual growth, risk-taking, and trust. Certainly teachers have opportunities to learn content, but how and in what conditions they learn both individually and together, how they share their practices, and even how they disagree is what constitutes a vibrant learning community. No one is resting on their laurels. Everyone supports one another. Critique is not something just for students, but for adults, too. Most of all, a primary goal of a professional learning community is raising student achievement.

One of the most important things that faculty and the leadership team have learned at BAA is that there must be regular and ongoing time for adults to talk to one another about their own work and the work of their students, and to observe one another teaching and then discuss those observations. Those are some of the important ingredients to create what we call a "professional learning community."

The story that follows about Camilla's first years of teaching at Boston Arts Academy contrasts significantly from Jocelyn's experiences. Although Camilla was feeling very real frustrations about her students and her own success, she had the support of her colleagues to talk and problem solve with her about her work. Furthermore, her job responsibilities are structured in such a way that she has the opportunity to see students in different venues than just her classroom, and she also works with a professional development partner from a different discipline, thus receiving and giving critical feedback.

Camilla's Story: A Math Teacher Learns from Her Colleagues and Her Students

As a beginning math teacher, Camilla felt the frustration of never "doing enough" for her students. Between correcting assignments, planning lessons, contacting parents, and meeting with individual students after school, not to mention general classroom management, the job seemed insurmountable. Camilla was determined to have her students work in groups on various math projects, and she was daunted by the lack of enthusiasm that many of her students exhibited in her first-period class. Her second-period class had no problem coming into the room and getting into groups

---

and getting down to business, but the first period . . . maybe it was because it was first thing in the morning. . . . Maybe it was because she wasn't a good enough teacher. . . . Maybe it was because this was a "bad" group of kids. Camilla had heard that theory before. A teacher could just get a "bad crop," and there was little one could do to improve the situation.

Although she had been trained in a teacher education program considered by many to be one of the best in the country, and she had learned about moving away from rote math learning into more inquiry based learning, little had prepared her for the flat looks of her students in first-period math.

"Just give us the worksheets," Laura would complain. "I don't want to be bothered working with Ian and Michaela."

In response, Camilla would insist: "The point is to work on these problems together. You will be describing your work to the rest of the class in a group, too. I am interested in how you solve problems together, not just that you get the answer."

Despite her best efforts to coach and explain, first period didn't seem to improve. When Camilla brought her disappointments to her math team meeting, her colleagues listened to her and helped problem solve. Some suggested that she had to be stricter with the first-period class. One teacher, who had taught some of the students before, said, "Some of those kids are used to getting away with stuff—especially Laura. She's a strong student and she doesn't ever like to slow down to explain anything to anyone. But she does want to get good grades. You have to remind her that this is part of her grade." Another teacher suggested that she watch some of the kids in their arts class. "They are mostly dancers, right?"

Camilla liked the idea of watching Ms. Chan's dance class. "Yeah, many of my students take Ms. Chan's modern class and Ms. Chan and I are professional development partners anyway, so I need to watch her teach. This would be a great reason! I want to see how Laura behaves there."

At a subsequent meeting, Camilla described her awe how she had watched her distracted math students excel in their modern dance classes. "First of all, Laura is the leader. She is right there in the front row in the

(Continued)

middle. She is super awake and she gets the combinations faster than anyone, sort of like in math." Ms. Chan explained that sometimes she puts Laura in a group with students who are as skilled as she is and sometimes the groups are more mixed. The other interesting thing is that Ian and Michaela are in that same class, too. But Laura isn't impatient with them there, even though they aren't as good technically. They're in a dance that Laura is choreographing. She seems to appreciate their expressiveness and willingness to take risks. The whole feeling is different from math class. The dance class starts with a set warm-up; then they work on some center floor routines; then they do across-the-floor work. The last part of class is more group work. I wonder about making my math class much more predictable. Almost set it up like dance class, and don't start with the group work. Watching their dance class structure makes me wonder about starting individually and quite independently and then introducing a new concept and then moving to group work. Maybe I won't get quite as much group time, but I think I'll have a more engaged class. Ms. Chan is coming in to visit my class next week. I'm sure we'll have other ideas after that, too.

"We also talked about ways to think about graphing functions through movement. I would love to see how I might connect some of the algebra that we are working on with the choreography projects Ms. Chan is beginning. That got me thinking about where the process of choreography is like learning mathematics."

The discussion among the math teachers went on and it was clear that Camilla would begin trying to see her students through a different lens—the lens of dance. She was open to how that experience might affect her as a math teacher. She was also pleased to see her students as successful learners in another discipline, namely dance, and she wanted to redouble her efforts to make math class and math learning more satisfying.

Much is known about what creates good schools and therefore high student achievement, but often the adult professional learning community is ignored. What accounts for Camilla's ultimate success with her students is a level of trust among colleagues. Camilla had learned to admit to needing help without fear of negative repercussions from her administration or peers. There is also time in the day to talk and think critically together about teaching and student success. Those conversations happen among the entire faculty as well as in smaller discipline and cross-discipline groups. Everyone is invested in student achievement—not just the math teachers. Teachers both within a discipline and between disciplines feed and support one another. There is openness to ask a question such as, "What can I do better to help my students become more successful mathematicians? Is there anything in the arts, or another discipline, that will help guide me?"

The role of peer observation is also important. Camilla has the chance to have a colleague, her professional development partner who is not an evaluator, visit her classroom and give her critical feedback. Although faculty and staff only do two required observations a year, which is not nearly enough, it is still a structured opportunity to have a colleague shed light on a teaching or work dilemma and offer nonevaluative insights or suggestions. Teachers often request someone from a particular discipline because they want to better understand how that discipline might connect to or be different from their own, and might enhance their progress on their professional goals. Camilla requested dance because she wanted to keep pursuing how dance students learn best and what about their approach to learning she might incorporate into her own classroom techniques.

At BAA teachers also have at least two or three views of the school. Camilla, for example, is a math teacher. She is also a dance advisor, and she teaches on the tenth grade seminar team. In this way, she has the opportunity to understand the school and her students through three lenses. She may see some of her math students as listless and uncooperative in her math class, but when she walks down the hall to dance class, she sees them exhibiting leadership, ingenuity, and creativity. Rather than become frustrated, she redoubles her efforts and asks, "What can I do better? How can I engage Laura more?" She also has an expectation that conversations in her team meetings can include opportunities to problem solve without judgment about her frustrations with her students. Feedback and support are forthcoming from many sectors of the school. She may even have the chance to develop a different curriculum after watching her students in dance class. She is willing and open to listening to her colleagues. And seeing her students in another arena certainly gives her renewed hope for their success in her classroom.

A few months after this particular class, Camilla had the opportunity to participate in a dance class, and this truly changed her students' view of her.

The fact that she was so willing to try their passion, and be a learner alongside her students, put them on a different playing field. One student that year even said to her, "Hey Ms. Nelson, you so willing to learn in our class, we gotta be better in your class." No words uttered by a student could have ever been sweeter.

Developing Schoolwide and Individual Goals and Strategies

I was fortunate enough to live through the genesis of a professional learning community at Fenway High School from the school's beginnings in the mid-1980s, and I brought those experiences with me to BAA. At Fenway, we developed a core foundation course called Social Issues that all teachers, no matter their primary content area, taught. We agreed early on that we would all teach the same units more or less at the same pace, and that we would implement many engaging large and small group activities. We agreed to regularly bring all our 200 students together in the cafeteria to read together, and many of the topics involved guest speakers. Social Issues was our shared place to plan and discuss both the content of the classes and how we would approach these controversial issues—in other words we had to discuss our teaching with each other. We also had to evaluate our students together, since we shared the same unit tests, and this meant that we were essentially critiquing one another. If one teacher's students did uniformly well we would ask: What did that teacher do to ensure such success with student learning? Conversely we also expressed concern if another teacher was less successful. How could we provide one another the support necessary so that all our students were learning the material more or less at the same level of proficiency? Over time, Social Issues became the way we defined our professional learning community, and it become our entry into talking about a range of issues in our school.

We all taught the class at the same time—first period—and all students took it. We offered the class first period as a way to "hook" students into arriving at school on time. (We had a terrible tardy issue.) Fifty percent of the curriculum focused on issues such as the Civil Rights Movement, bussing in Boston, the war in El Salvador, and nuclear proliferation. The other 50%, designed by students, dealt with issues of concern to adolescent development such as violence, sexuality, music, or friendship.

We had to agree on how we would present issues such as Boston's school desegregation case, which was still very raw for many families and teachers. And we needed to be very thoughtful and strategic about lessons related HIV/AIDS, since this was in the mid-1980s when the epidemic was just breaking. We were also a very diverse group of teachers from many different persuasions in terms of religion, social class, and racial backgrounds. It wasn't easy to construct the common units and the accompanying assessments that we could all do together. Although we only had two 40-minute periods a week to plan the curriculum and assessments, many of us stayed late in the afternoon to ensure that our lessons were well-crafted. Furthermore, we needed the time together to talk about how our students were faring.

A professional learning community needs nurturing and leadership. I was in charge of the development of the Social Issues curriculum. This meant that I could prepare materials for the rest of the team to critique and adapt at our weekly meetings. I did this for a number of years until other teachers felt comfortable taking the leadership of developing units for others to use. We had established a level of trust among one another so that we could share the responsibility of developing curriculum.

The Social Issues course provided the opportunity for us to see how our students were assimilating information and understanding across teachers' classes. The majority of students in all ten Social Issues classes performed similarly on unit assessments, but there was one class in which the students always did poorly. We had to try to figure out why this was so.

We had teachers who had been assigned to our school but had chosen not to teach there. One teacher, who was nearing the end of his career, regularly missed school days during horse racing season. He owned a racetrack and many horses, and essentially had two jobs. Although he always had doctors' notes excusing his absences, it was very disruptive for students and for the school. His Social Issues class was often left without a teacher, and the students were angry, since they had become invested in the topics we were studying. We tried to make do with substitute teachers, but that was not reliable. Sometimes I would merge his class with mine, but it was difficult to have a sustained conversation with 50 students in the room. We tried to talk with the absentee teacher about ways to improve his attendance. We wanted him to understand how his behavior was eroding our professional learning community and students' fledgling sense of community, and, most important, undermining student achievement. His students were the least prepared for the end of unit exams because they missed so many classes. And his students were the least engaged in the curriculum, since their classroom discussions were so erratic.

Finally, we made a decision as a faculty that we would ask his student teacher to take over his class and we would provide the student teacher with a stipend. (We had a small grant to support the curriculum development for Social Issues and we asked the grant maker if we could divert the money this way.) Although this would mean that none of the teachers would receive a stipend to continue our after-school planning work, all the teachers preferred working voluntarily in order to ensure that all students had their own class. We decided that it was more of a hardship for us to have an unprepared substitute teacher or to combine two classes than to forego the money. We did not have to allow an external situation that seemed beyond our control to destroy our fledgling professional learning community or our students' achievement.

Making the MEAL: BAA Writing Seminar

When I had the chance to open BAA, I felt that a similar experience of everyone teaching a core class would be beneficial to the development of our professional learning community. I had seen the power of a core course at Fenway, but I didn't know what that course would be at BAA. In the Spring before BAA officially opened with students, we had a series of meetings with a range of participants—artists, academics, community members, parents, college students. We asked the same question at each meeting: "What should BAA graduates know and be able to do?" Although a range of answers always surfaced, there was always one common response: "BAA graduates had to know how to write a grant. Artists live and die by grants." That was our motivation to begin our schoolwide approach to writing. Teaching writing would be the foundation of our professional learning community.

We decided that all teachers would co-teach writing seminar and all students would take it, and at the same time of the day. Co-teaching would create a natural pairing for professional development partners. Teachers would observe one another in writing class and then in the teacher's primary curriculum area as well. Through this writing class we would build a common vocabulary for writing that would permeate all of our classes. We incorporated an acronym from other educators called MEAL—main idea, evidence, analysis, link—that provides students with a formula for writing a paragraph or the famed five-paragraph essay for our state's standardized test. Seminar became the place to develop and practice a schoolwide approach to teaching and assessment.

Under the wise and careful guidance of our curriculum coordinator, Anne Clark, our grade level writing seminar class became the central place for professional development. Ms. Clark's role was particularly important for our emerging professional learning community. She was our resident literacy "expert" and knew all the current educational literature about how to improve students' literacy skills. She is also an excellent teacher. Her job was to plan lessons with and for teachers; watch teachers teach and then give critical feedback, and teach a particular lesson or skill that a teacher felt unsure about how to introduce. She was always open and eager to have teachers critique her as well.

Ms. Clark convened and led discussions about seminar so we could create a schoolwide rubric for judging good writing, and also connect that rubric to our Habits of the Graduate. These habits are akin to the "Habits of Mind" described by the educational philosopher John Dewey—the orientation toward learning that we wish our graduates to demonstrate. These habits form an intellectual framework that our students and staff use in every classroom, arts and academic. They represent the best aspects of both the artistic and academic processes. We sometimes refer to them by the acronym RICO: refine, invent, connect, and own. She provided exemplars of student writing so that we could agree on what constituted proficient writing. By scoring student writing individually as teachers, as co-teaching pairs, and finally as grade-level teams, we developed shared teacher accountability. Accountability is a much bandied about word today in the education reform literature, but we were engaging in this process long before it became in vogue. We had to learn to question one another if one teacher gave a student a very high grade on the writing rubric and another did not. If a teaching pair didn't share similar views on what constituted good writing, that wasn't fair to students. We spent many hours collaboratively grading work and then discussing why we had given a certain grade. Over time we would reach consensus. We continue to do this ongoing reading and grading of student work together. This requires time, leadership, and trust, but it is critical for the health of a sustained professional community.

Our original premise, which I think still holds true, is that it is less threatening for teachers to develop a set of shared expectations and practices for a course that everyone teaches but that is no one's primary content area. None of us were writing experts, except Ms. Clark and one or two others. What mattered for our students' success is that we all grew to share a similar philosophy and understanding of what constituted good work in writing and how to teach those skills. By doing this intense work together for writing seminar, we could then transfer these skills to other content areas. For example, now all classes use a MEAL format for writing a short essay. Questions about how we would reflect RICO in the writing portfolio became relevant for assessment discussions in other subjects. Essentially, by having a schoolwide discussion related to assessment in writing, we were learning to have that discussion in many other areas.

In seminar, teachers were given a choice to teach from the curriculum that we developed or to teach the same "big ideas" but with their own creativity. In this way, we created the menu, but allowed teachers to pick and choose both approach and content. Everyone had to do a persuasive essay, but each teacher could approach this assignment differently. Clearly, it is not always easy for teachers to reach consensus on content (standards) and assessment (how students do). Often it means that a teacher has to give up a favorite lesson or reading for the sake of a cohesive team. Nonetheless, our experience has demonstrated that this kind of commitment to a professional learning community will increase student achievement.

As we scored student work together and team-taught in writing seminar, we also identified skills that we needed to further develop as teachers. Since our auditions are academically blind, we have a very broad range of students in our classrooms. Many have learning disabilities and receive special education services. Others struggle to complete assignments and read two to four grades below average. Still others are reading at the college level. Early on we recognized that we needed to improve our teachers' skills to effectively teach in heterogeneous classrooms, without boring our highly-skilled students or frustrating students challenged by learning issues. We put a number of initiatives in place simultaneously.

Deepening Professional Practice

Friday faculty meetings are primarily for professional development. We read texts together that expand our understanding of terms such as "differentiated instruction" or "heterogeneous groupings." We discuss classroom-based examples from the literature of such instruction. We debate whether and how these examples would work in our setting. We also discuss our own classroom experiences, often by sharing our written observations of one another. At certain points along the year, we do a more in-depth sharing and critiquing of one another's practices. This is always a favorite opportunity for teachers to share a practice that has been particularly successful or one in which they need their colleagues' critical appraisal.

We have also taken graduate level courses together during faculty meeting time. Topics have included learning disabilities; behavioral challenges to learning; and reading at the secondary level with special attention to cultural, racial, linguistic, and gender influences on literacy development. Over time we are increasing our abilities and skills in heterogeneous classroom teaching. For example, we have developed strategies and systems such as Open Honors to address the needs of both struggling and more skilled students. We have learned how to look at a text and figure out its level of reading difficulty and how to adapt a college level text to a ninth grade reading level.

We have spent, and continue to spend, professional time together to better understand the difference between functional and cultural literacy. Although it is important to understand the phonemic structures of reading and where students with poor skills may stumble, teachers also must understand, as Freire so aptly describes in *Pedagogy of the Oppressed,* how cultural literacy can increase reading skills. However, promoting cultural literacy does not just mean finding texts that directly connect to students' own experiences, but rather finding methods of teaching so that Aristotle and Shakespeare and Oscar Wilde connect to students' experiences. This is not a simple task. We were determined not to fall prey to the practice often seen in schools with poor readers whereby students are only given texts from their own cultural backgrounds. Students who had never heard of the Ancient Greeks began to spout Aristotle and Sophocles as if they were a friend from around the corner. As teachers, this meant that we were grappling with how to teach difficult texts successfully.

As we better understood functional and cultural literacy, we realized that to be effective in the classroom, we needed to ground our professional learning community within the diverse experiences of our students and families. That meant that our faculty needed to know where our students came from. We felt that this was part of being culturally literate teachers.

Getting to Know Our Students' Neighborhoods

One year, before school started we went on a bus tour to our students' neighborhoods. Various faculty members from those neighborhoods narrated the tours and discussed the history from many perspectives. We learned where the vibrant jazz and blues scene had started in Boston. We visited some of the oldest community centers and boys and girls clubs in the country. We visited some of the nation's most historic markers on the Black History Trail. At the same time we saw and discussed many positive neighborhood institutions, new developments, and wonderful examples of urban renewal, we also saw some of the conditions of neighborhoods that have been blighted by drugs and gang activity. Whenever we saw one of our students, either hanging out in a local park (it was summer still, after all) or painting a mural as part of a community mural project, we got off the bus to greet them. Some students literally gasped when they saw all 50 of their teachers trooping off a bus to say "hi" at a historic Roxbury park or street corner, but others loved the fact that their teachers were coming to check out where they lived. For the teachers, particularly those who had not grown up in urban areas, this visit was a critical part of understanding the neighborhoods and backgrounds of their students.

As our foundational course that everyone worked on together, Seminar gave teachers opportunity after opportunity to take on schoolwide problems together. Through our work in seminar we debated how to better prepare our students to be successful on state high-stakes tests such as MCAS (Massachusetts Comprehensive Assessment System) or college entrance exams such as SATs. We also worked on developing interdisciplinary units, and that led to a commitment to deepen our own understanding of how we defined the term *interdisciplinary*. We struggled to improve our students' abstract thinking skills, and we explored ways to have all our students know more about arts history outside their own major. As our discussions became more focused and where we were stuck became clearer, we realized that this process of talking, debating, critiquing, sharing, and reflecting was the way that our schoolwide goals emerged.

Our schoolwide goals are the underpinning for our professional learning community. The goals that emerge are the dilemmas we take on each year. However, unlike typical district mandates that might change with the political winds, these goals have consistently focused on our efforts to increase student achievement across racial, gender, and socioeconomic backgrounds. The word choice may shift or deepen from year to year, but the intentions have remained the same. Teachers, too, write individual professional development plans using the schoolwide goals. Students and parents and caregivers also discuss these goals. Bringing them into the dialogue about how to increase student achievement can ensure that all constituents feel part of the school's professional learning community. Before teachers do their peer observations, they review one another's professional development plans and try to connect their observations to the areas in which their partner wanted to improve. The schoolwide goals, the faculty professional development plans, and the peer observations are all specific activities to promote a strong professional learning community.

Retaining Teachers: The Importance of Community

Finally, and this may be one of the most important features of BAA's professional learning community, there are multiple opportunities for teachers to take risks in their classrooms with curriculum. Teachers are willing to try new techniques or use new materials because they are not worried about reprisals or punishments because there is trust between our teachers and administration. It is acceptable to make mistakes. There may be criticism about practices, encouragements to change or adapt, from both colleagues and supervisors, but there is no harsh judgment that a teacher is bad if he or she has tried a new lesson or introduced a whole new project. Furthermore, a professional learning community is an important tool in teacher retention and early career development. Jocelyn has already left teaching, but Camilla is still in the profession, as is our science teacher Emily Jong.

Emily's Story: A Science Teacher Learns from an Administrator

Emily Jong sat slumped and exhausted in Ms. Torres's office. "I just feel like nothing I do is right. I can't get through to Ashley. I'm not sure I can get through to Janet either." Her face was crestfallen. Her shoulders were hunched, and she looked like she carried too much pain for her twenty-five years.

(Continued)

Earlier in the day, Ms. Jong had participated in Janet's suspension hearing. Both girls had been suspended because following Ms. Jong's science class experiment with cell phones and what materials might block a cell phone signal, a brawl had broken out after school. "I didn't think for a minute that the activity would lead to so much drama. When Jeff [security] came to me and explained that he had both girls in separate student support team offices because they had gone at it after class, I was just shocked.

"'You know,' he said to me, 'Well, we don't allow cell phones in schools, and class was an opportunity to see who they each had on their lists and sure enough both girls had Angel and that caused suspicion, and a whole he said–she said thing. That turned into a fight.' I heard something in class about Ashley asking Janet why she had Angel's number, but I didn't think anything about it. I was just excited that everyone was engaged in the experiment using tin foil. I didn't realize it would cause such controversy and eruptions later. I feel so terrible. This was really my fault. Maybe I just don't know how to connect with this population. I didn't grow up with any of the pressures that Ashley or Janet has. I never questioned authority; never thought of hitting another kid in school or outside of school. I would have probably been thrown out of my house if I did that. It just wasn't part of my culture. In my family, growing up and going to college was a given—you know, a stereotypical Asian family. Play an instrument, do well in school, and go to college. Maybe I just don't understand Janet and Ashley. I sometimes wonder if I'm what they need as a teacher. They may have beautiful voices, but how will they ever do in college. They haven't even turned in any lab reports. They are failing my class!"

Ms. Torres listened and calmed Ms. Jong down. "You are the right teacher for our kids, Emily. You are an excellent teacher. You are incredibly creative. You know your content. Now maybe I wouldn't have used cell phones as an experiment given that we say kids aren't allowed to have their cell phones visible in school, but you couldn't have known that they would fight. Sure, maybe you should have been more attuned to the culture of that class, and the tensions brewing, but you did your best. That is the most we can all ask from ourselves. We'll set up a mediation for them when they come back from suspension. We'll also have them create a contract about how they will behave in your class. And before they come back into your classroom, as we discussed this morning in the hearing, they will have to write a letter of apology. It is not OK to interrupt the learning of others. Ever. They violated 'community with social responsibility,' our shared values. They are both on the Student Support Team's radar as kids we need to watch. We know that there are lots of other issues going on with both of them—separately and individually. I can't even get a parent up here for Ashley's hearing."

Ms. Torres was still focused on the lessons she was trying to teach the students, but Ms. Jong, as a second-year teacher, had different priorities.

"I'm just embarrassed that I can't control my own class," Ms. Jong admitted.

Ms. Torres responded firmly. "You can. This was a difficult situation. You are still learning about classroom management. I'll bring Janet back into class on Friday, and see that everything goes smoothly. A Student Support Team member will also stop by every day through the end of the week. This isn't for you to solve alone. That's why I'm here and Student Support, and even Ms. Montes, Janet's advisor. This is something we all will work on together."

An interaction between teacher and administrator occurs too infrequently in many urban high schools. In too many schools, it is solely the responsibility of the classroom teacher to work out altercations or even fights. Too often there is rarely sustained administrative involvement or oversight in altercations. The reasons for these shortcomings can be many and varied. There are too many students in a school to deal with each case carefully and thoughtfully; there are too few student support or administrative personnel to provide helpful interventions; there are too few alternatives for students who need a different kind of classroom environment. There is altogether too little support for teachers like Ms. Emily Jong, and good teachers, like her, leave the profession prematurely. A professional learning community that embraces everyone, such as we have struggled to create at BAA, can be a lifeline for veteran and beginning teachers, administrators, students, and even parents.

Too often teachers like Ms. Jong would never feel comfortable enough going to their administrator for help, but she and Ms. Torres co-taught writing seminar together the previous year, and she has also seen Ms. Torres struggle to reach a student. Whatever the reasons for the lack of support in many schools, too often students like Ashley and Janet end up right back in the classroom after a brief suspension with little progress having been made to resolve their disagreements that brought about the suspension. Often the classroom teacher has not been involved or appraised of any of the issues or repercussions and is just expected to go on teaching like nothing ever occurred. And too often student altercations are not part of any sustained teaching about appropriate behavior or building of a shared school culture and a positive whole-school professional community.

Ms. Torres may not have agreed with Ms. Jong's choice of a lesson for her students, but she certainly doesn't blame Ms. Jong for trying a new idea. She may question Ms. Jong's judgment, and wish that she had consulted with her or others on her team about her "innovative lesson," but Ms. Torres is committed to creating a culture in which teaching practices are seen as continuing endeavors in improvement.

If teachers (and students) don't feel encouraged to try new techniques or assignments, readings, lab experiments, and so forth that might not work the first time, why would teachers or students, or parents for that matter, ever trust that they, in fact, had a stake or responsibility in the outcomes of any decisions? Although Ms. Jong feels discouraged, and even wonders aloud if she has the stuff it takes to be successful in urban education, she knows she has Ms. Torres's support and the support of her team members. The next time she does this lesson, she perhaps will think differently about what materials to use, and even about how to group students. In fact, her entire science team will spend time going over one another's lesson just to be on the lookout for lessons that might backfire. But even if students erupt because of outside issues that have nothing to do with the lesson, Ms. Jong knows that the school will "have her back." She will not be left out in the cold to manage both lesson planning and classroom management alone. There is trust. There is a strong professional learning community.

Ms. Jong presents an example of a new teacher who has learned that taking risks and being vulnerable about her practice is accepted and expected. Veteran teachers are also willing to make mistakes and share their challenges with their peers. The strength of Boston Arts Academy is that no matter how seasoned a teacher you are, everyone is always learning. That is what risk-taking is about—pushing one's own learning to another level and being willing to try something different that just might be terrifically successful, or not.

Building Buy-in for Professional Learning Communities

My colleagues in other schools talk about their disappointments with how small groups of teachers can often filibuster to such an extent that decisions or action steps that would improve achievement for the majority of students never occur. Schools often get derailed in their pursuit of increased student achievement and the advancement of a professional learning community because the buy-in on the part of all teachers is lacking. This is intensely frustrating, but it must be reckoned with. This was the threat we faced at Fenway in the early stages of the school's development with the teacher (and racetrack owner) whose negative behavior nearly toppled all of our work. We worked creatively and hard to figure out a way to marginalize his impact on our students. It was not easy.

Nonetheless, I maintain that if school leaders can hold steadfastly to strategies that increase trust and risk-taking among teachers, while simultaneously increasing teachers' technical skills and overall pedagogy, professional learning communities can emerge and be sustained. The struggle is maintaining this balance of teacher skill enhancement while also instituting practices such as schoolwide professional development goals and peer observations to increase that teacher to teacher trust.

One of the ways BAA found success was through a schoolwide focus on a core course-writing seminar. Not all schools must have all teachers teach a schoolwide writing class, but all schools, particularly secondary schools, might do well to consider what kinds of schoolwide courses and experiences could be offered and taught by all teachers in order to engender a professional learning community. The new favorite trend of Small Learning Communities that are often organized around a particular theme, such as media, technology, or health, might find that instituting a core course taught by all and taken by all could provide the foundation upon which a professional learning community could flourish.

In order to be successful with students, teachers need to feel safe to ask for help from colleagues. Asking for help was an expectation in seminar at BAA. None of us were experts. None of us could do it alone. In meeting after meeting, we could share our worries and frustrations. Besides Ms. Clark's expert assistance, even Ms. Torres and I taught seminar in the early years, and we struggled along with the teachers. It was important that we, too, could admit frustration and failure. Asking for help requires trust, and this is a key ingredient for a vibrant professional learning community.

Lessons Learned

There are many kinds of communities that might emerge in schools. Teachers might feel emotionally connected to one another and supportive of one another's personal development. It is quite common in schools that adults want to know about how colleagues spent their weekends or whether family members are well, or who just had a baby or got married. There is nothing wrong with these kinds of concerns, but it is not the same as a professional learning community. A professional learning community is one in which teachers have time to share, write, and talk about their teaching and their students in ways that are very focused and reflective. When such a community is absent, teaching is a solitary activity, all too often leading to bad results for teachers and students. A school with a healthy professional learning community will keep a razor-sharp focus on student achievement, and faculty will feel a common ownership and responsibility for that achievement. When such a community is present it can be the key to an entire school's success.

Reflection Questions

1. What kind of professional conversations take place among teachers in your school?

2. What opportunities exist for teachers to collaborate to make up courses and objectives?

3. Do you think that allowing for the level of collaboration and support that exists at Boston Arts Academy would help with retaining new teachers?

Resources

Benitez, M., Davidson, J., Flaxman, L., Sizer, T., & Sizer, N. (2009). *Small Schools, Big Ideas: The Essential Guide to Successful School Transformation.* San Francisco: Jossey-Bass.

DiMartino, J., & Clarke, J. (2004). Personal prescription for engagement. *Principal Leadership, 4*(8).

DiMartino, J., & Clarke, J. (2008). *Personalizing the High School Experience for Each Student.* Alexandria, VA: ASCD.

DiMartino, J., Clarke, J., & Wolk, D. (eds.) (2003). *Personalized Learning: Preparing High School Students to Create Their Futures.* Lanham, MD: Rowman & Littlefield.

Nathan, L. (2009). *The Hardest Questions Aren't on the Test: Lessons from an Innovative Urban School.* Boston: Beacon Press.

Integrating Student Leadership

A Personalized Approach to Rigor

Jeff Park

Front Range Early College High School, Denver, Colorado

What would happen if we threw out all the rules we know about high school? What if we got rid of bell schedules and course descriptions, ignored seat time requirements and scope and sequence, marginalized textbooks and testing, saw teachers as learners and not subject area experts, and used the school building as only one location for learning? What if we instead framed learning around interests and passions, used the world as the classroom, and expected every student to prepare for college? Could we create the kinds of small, personalized high schools we know our students need and our communities deserve?

In response to this last question, Dennis Littky and Elliott Washor opened The Met School in Providence, Rhode Island, in fall 1996. What they pioneered at The Met has come to be known as the Big Picture school design, one of the dozen or so innovative high school designs chosen for national replication by the Bill & Melinda Gates Foundation's high school initiative. In the time since The Met first opened its doors, the work of Littky and Washor has influenced state legislation and policy, seen a host of imitators, and led to the creation of more than 40 replica schools across the country. At the same time, the Big Picture design has led to thousands of students having rigorous personalized learning experiences customized to help them reach their goals, address their needs, and enhance their strengths. And it has seen hundreds of students from minority- and high-poverty backgrounds, many of them first-generation high school graduates, go on to college.

In this chapter, we look at how the components of the Big Picture design combine to create rigorous, personalized learning for every student. We'll look at how students, teachers, parents, and mentors work together to frame the learning. And we'll examine a case study of one student's education to learn how learning plans, project planning, internships, and exhibitions are all employed to create learning that achieves a level of rigor not found in a typical high school classroom.

Dylan's Story

Everything that I can remember in school before I started at Big Picture had been a big problem. All throughout middle school no one would pay attention to me. The teachers thought that they had "too much" to deal with, and gave me no time to talk with them. I believe that a lot of them thought that it was simply just easier to ignore me because I was going to fail anyway.

Dylan, a recent Met graduate

Like many high school educators, I became a teacher because I wanted to change the system. Partly because my own high school experience had been difficult, and partly out of a sense of social justice, I entered the ranks as a high school humanities teacher in an urban school in Denver, Colorado. It was 1994, and the state had just adopted content standards in the major subject areas. I taught social studies on an integrated ninth grade "Core" team with license to innovate as much as we needed in order to have our students reach the standards. So it was in those rarified circumstances that I began to explore high school teaching and learning.

That first year, my partners, a language arts teacher and a science teacher, and I shared planning time and a common group of 90 students. We also had one guidance counselor assigned to our 90 kids, and one administrator exclusive to the Core. We taught in a three-period block, so we had nearly 160 minutes to use flexibly.

We had fun exploring the variety that these structures allowed us. We taught integrated units. We ability-grouped to help students develop basic skills. We pieced out assignments to one another. We gave integrated assessments. We moved kids from one cohort to another. In essence, we did whatever we felt the circumstances warranted. It was a lot of fun, but in the end, all of our creativity seemed to have very little effect on achievement.

Over the next five years, I continued to teach on a Core team. Eventually we added a math teacher, expanded to 120 students, and worked over five periods, including lunch. We had a special education teacher join the team. We looped with the students from ninth to tenth grade. And we continued to integrate. In my final year in the classroom, 1999, students who had been in the looped Core for two years showed marginal gains on the CTB test (Colorado's standardized assessment) over students in the general population. Not the huge results we'd hoped for, but some confirmation that the consistency and stability we'd provided for those students had made a difference.

By no means did I feel like we'd figured out how to improve achievement in a large comprehensive high school. And there were plenty of things we didn't or weren't able to do, including using ongoing formative assessments to make decisions. We didn't involve parents all that well, and hadn't the resources we would have needed to expand learning outside of the classroom. But it was a start, and that year our principal was selected as the state Principal of the Year, in large part because of the innovation his leadership had fostered.

For the next three years, I worked in a central office position in teaching and learning, and also worked as a consultant on high school reform through a federally funded regional educational laboratory. I continued to learn about the best ways to "keep school" and was bound and determined to make a difference in public education.

Then in 2002, I got the best educational leadership gig going: I was hired by the Big Picture Company, Inc., and the Colorado Small Schools Initiative (CSSI) to start a small high school in Denver modeled after the Met Center in Providence, Rhode Island. My project was funded by a national replication grant to Big Picture from the Bill & Melinda Gates Foundation, as well as by a Gates facilitation grant to CSSI, and local funding from the Piton Foundation, the Stapleton Foundation, the Walton Family Foundation, and the Rose Community Foundation. I've been fortunate enough to open three Big Picture schools in Denver: Skyland Community High School (opened in 2003), a charter school in Denver Public Schools; and Mapleton Preparatory High School (2004) and Front Range Early College (2005), both in Mapleton Public

Schools, in the north Denver metro area. I'm currently the school director at Mapleton Prep and Front Range Early College.

A Big Picture school represents the cutting edge in school redesign, because it throws off all of the confines of the traditional comprehensive high school. Gone are routines like bell schedules and 55-minute classes. Instead the day is broken up into flexible chunks of time that foster real-world exploration and independent work time. Teachers, called advisors, work with a small cohort of students (usually no more than 18) and loop with their students from year to year. There is no course catalog of requirements; it is replaced by an individual learning plan customized to each student's strengths, needs, and goals. Tests give way to authentic assessments, including demonstration of learning through exhibitions, student reflection through narrative writing, and panels evaluating student work in a learning team. Interests and passions are the catalyst for subject area learning, and every student is expected to apply to college.

The New 3 Rs of High School Education

In this small environment, we've deliberately created a set of structures and practices that enable us to offer a learning environment that embodies the new 3 Rs: rigor, relevance, and relationship. These three ideals rose to national attention when the Bill & Melinda Gates Foundation claimed them and made them the key elements for the reforms they hoped to catalyze through philanthropy. Just a quick survey of the literature on small high schools reveals that these terms have reached a level of ubiquity that obscures their provenience, and indeed makes their origins unimportant.

Relevance is at the heart of everything we do in a Big Picture school. We plan student learning based on it, we create community-based learning experiences to enhance it, and we use methods of assessment that require students to talk about it. Very little of what we do is imposed on students because of some arbitrary set of requirements; instead, we place a high value on creating learning experiences that are relevant to student interests, passions, and needs.

Relationships are also an integral part of how we view teaching and learning at a Big Picture school. Nowhere is this more evident than in the Learning Plan

Team, the core group of adults, including parent, teacher, and mentor, who partner together to manage the individual student's learning.

Rigor, however, is much more of a moving target in a Big Picture school. We believe that the structures and expectations we have in place at our school lead to learning that is more rigorous than that found in most high school classes. But we also have a take on rigor that may differ from how others view it.

Rigor is a loaded term, one influenced by the subtleties of context. Consider some synonyms:

Rigor can mean "strict," like the Military Code of Discipline, a set of rules and guidelines that is designed to be followed to the letter.

Rigor can mean "difficult," like Michelangelo painting the Sistine Chapel, a process that required the artist to spend years on his back, on scaffolding, to accomplish his masterpiece.

Rigor can mean "traditional," like a high school chemistry class, with its lectures, precise formulas, and meticulous procedures.

Rigor can mean "severe," like the stereotypical parochial school with teachers with paddles meant to impose discipline.

Rigor can mean "inflexible," like the petty bureaucracy of an enforcement agency like the Internal Revenue Service.

None of those definitions seem to fit the idea of improving high school, nor do they describe what the typical Big Picture student achieves over and over again. So consider two alternative definitions of rigor:

Rigor: "the goal of helping students develop the capacity to understand content that is *complex, ambiguous, provocative,* and *personally* or *emotionally challenging*" (R. McCarthy)

Rigor: learning that causes students to take some type of action, to develop their own questions, to notice, observe, and retain, to learn how hard it is to do something well (E. Washor and C. Mojowski)

It is this context, one that encourages complexity, is active, and requires evolution in the learner, that we strive to create in a Big Picture school.

Overview: The School Design

At a Big Picture school, a series of key components come together to create learning that is both personalized and rigorous.

Component 1: Teaching and Learning

Advisory

This is a core student group of between 15 and 18 students that serves as a student's home base and center of accountability. Each advisory stays together with a single advisor (teacher) for two to four years. The intimacy of such a small group allows for student-to-advisor interaction that is unparalleled in other school structures. It also provides every student with a set of peers who support, challenge, and help one another to reach their fullest potential.

Advisors

Teachers in a Big Picture school are called advisors, and each advisor is responsible for the educational experience of their advisees. Advisors manage each student's personal schedule and Learning Plan (described below), and acts as direct links to family and internship mentors. Advisors get to know the whole student, not just his or her ability in one subject area. Advisors do not teach formal classes but are integrally involved in each student's learning process. The advisors conduct advisory meetings, work individually with each student, and sometimes teach workshops to students interested in a particular topic. They also help set up and oversee student internships, facilitate Learning Plan meetings, and provide guidance through student exhibitions.

Pick Me Ups

Three times a week, the entire school gathers in the morning for a community meeting called Pick Me Up (PMU). Students, mentors, and visitors give short presentations that help students explore and present their interests and build a sense of community. The PMUs uplift, stimulate, and inspire the school community, as well as showcase the diverse talents of all students.

Learning Plans

Each student works together with his or her Learning Plan Team—made up of parents, internship mentor, and advisor—to develop a Learning Plan.

Learning Goals

The Learning Plan is aligned to five Learning Goals, and students must demonstrate proficiency in each area. Each Learning Goal incorporates components of traditional subject areas and aligns to state and district standards. Table 8.1 illustrates this.

There are additional grade level goals that must also be incorporated into each Learning Plan. The plan is revised every trimester and sets the expectations for the student's work, learning, and skill building. Learning Plans are always built around exploring the student's interests and finding natural ways to integrate the Learning Goals. Each Learning Plan centers around individual projects, workshops offered at school, and community-based learning opportunities (e.g., internship, college class, volunteerism).

Component 2: Learning Through Internship

Big Picture students are actively engaged in the world in meaningful and productive ways, and their learning is as "real" and applicable to everyday life as possible. A central way this engagement is made possible is through workplace internships called LTIs (Learning Through Internship). LTIs are the core of a student's Learning Plan and are chosen based on students' interests and passions. Unlike vocational education, LTIs integrate school-based learning with

Table 8.1. Learning Goals and Standards

Big Picture Learning Goal	Traditional Subject Areas	Sample Standards Alignment
Empirical reasoning: to use empirical evidence and logical process to make decisions and evaluate hypotheses.	Science, math, computer science	**Colorado Science Standard 1.0:** Students understand the processes of scientific investigation and design, conduct, communicate about, and evaluate such investigations.
Quantitative analysis: to understand numbers, analyze uncertainty, comprehend the properties of shapes, and study how things change over time.	Math, computer science	**Colorado Math Standard 3.0:** Data Analysis—Students use data collection and analysis, statistics, and probability in problem-solving situations and communicate the reasoning used in solving these problems.
Communication: to understand your audience, to write, read, speak, and listen well, to use technology and artistic expression to communicate, and to be exposed to another language.	Reading, writing, visual and performing arts, foreign languages	**Colorado Reading and Writing Standard 3.0:** Students write and speak using formal grammar, usage, sentence structure, punctuation, capitalization, and spelling.
Social reasoning: to see diverse perspectives, to understand social issues, to explore ethics, and to look at issues historically.	Social studies	**Colorado History Standard 1.0:** Students understand the chronological organization of history and know how to organize events and people into major eras to identify and explain historical relationships.
Personal qualities: to demonstrate respect, leadership, responsibility, organization, and time management and to reflect on your abilities and strive to improve.	Physical education, health, character education	**Colorado Physical Education Standard 4.0:** Students understand the importance of physical activity and its contribution to a healthy lifestyle.

workplace learning. Starting in the ninth grade, students attend their LTIs two days a week, where they learn through one-on-one mentoring and project exploration. And at school, advisors reinforce the skills and knowledge needed to complete the student's projects. The aim is to provide students with learning opportunities linked to their interests that help them develop academic and interpersonal skills and that help them become good citizens of the community. Thus, LTIs at an engineering firm, a doctor's office, a machine shop, a glassblower's studio, a retail store, a graphic designer, or a community-based organization would all provide equally valid experiences for students.

Component 3: Authentic Assessment

Assessment is a key area for Big Picture schools. Students must thoroughly document their work to determine whether they are fulfilling their Learning Plans. Elements of assessment include the following:

Learning Goals

The Learning Goals are a series of academic and personal goals that constitute the expectations for each student. Students set Learning Goals each quarter.

Exhibitions

Each trimester, students present an exhibition of their learning to a panel of parents, students, teachers, and others. The exhibitions give students the opportunity to present evidence of learning, demonstration of mastery of skills and knowledge, and progress made on the Learning Plan.

Narratives

Big Picture schools promote a culture of writing in which every student and staff member actively seeks to become a proficient writer. Following each Exhibition, advisors write one- to two-page descriptions of the student's progress throughout the trimester. Students write personal narratives reflecting on their Exhibition. These documents serve two purposes: first, they become entries in the student's portfolio (described below), and second, they become evidence of academic progress. Narratives take the place of letter grades, providing much deeper analyses of the student's work, personal and academic accomplishments, and areas for improvement.

Portfolios

Students must thoroughly document their work and learning through building portfolios. We use carefully structured portfolios as an occasion for learning. There are four types of portfolios used at a Big Picture school, each having a clearly articulated framework. The Working Portfolio contains all of the student's current Learning Plan work. The Portfolio Box archives finished projects and drafts of writing. Final Presentation Portfolios are created at the end of the year and show growth through the year and examples of best work. Seniors create College Portfolios, smaller, professionally presented compilations of the student's résumé, transcripts, recommendations, awards, and best work; this portfolio is used when applying for further education or career opportunities.

Gateway Requirements

To prove that they are ready to enter the second half of their Big Picture education, called Senior Institute, students at the end of their second year must fulfill the Gateway Requirements. This includes giving a preliminary in-depth exhibition during which students present a special portfolio to a select panel, revising the work in the portfolio based on questions and suggestions from the panel, and presenting a second exhibition. The second presentation must include four letters of recommendation, a completed Final Presentation Portfolio of work from the initial exhibition, a final reflective essay explaining why the student is ready for Senior Institute, and an interview with the same select panel.

Graduation Requirements

In addition to completing the curricular requirements aligned to district policy, there are specific graduation requirements for seniors. First, each student must write a 50–75 page autobiography that includes a chapter on the student's experiences at the school. Seniors must also complete a Senior Thesis Project, which involves a large, integrated, challenging project through which the student gives back to the community. As part of the Senior Thesis Project, students must also write a 15-page, fully cited, formatted thesis. Seniors must also go through college preparation and application, where they compile their college portfolios, take the ACT and/or SAT, complete financial aid and scholarship applications, and take at least one college class while in high school. Finally, each potential graduate must complete the 18 learning goals at their grade level. These include things like demonstrating heightened personal qualities and depth of work, playing a leadership role in school, and reading at least one book a month.

Component 4: Family Engagement

At a Big Picture school, we don't just enroll kids, we enroll families. Families are a vital part of the school community and are encouraged to become actively involved. Families are a student's primary teacher, so families are considered partners in educating one student at a time.

Learning Plan Team

At least one parent or guardian must be part of each student's Learning Plan Team, which meets four times a year. For students whose parents aren't able to be part of the Learning Plan Team, then a concerned adult—an older sibling, an aunt or uncle, or an adult friend, for example—can attend instead.

Communication with Parents

Advisors are in close contact with parents and communicate with them whenever needed. Home visits, picnics, letters, phone calls, and e-mails are all effective tools for family–school communication.

Family Engagement Committee

Our school has a group of active parents who help establish a family-oriented environment at the school through a variety of activities and trips. Activities of the committee also includes a parent "buddy system" to orient families who are new to our school.

Community Events

Throughout the school year, family engagement events are held. These events serve as celebrations for the community at large, culture building and information sharing forums, and community outreach programs.

Component 5: Flexibility

Big Picture students enjoy an unparalleled level of personalized education. Through advisory and LTI, students develop close, personal relationships with caring adults, both experienced educators and seasoned professionals. Because

Table 8.2. A Typical Big Picture Student Learning Experience

	Monday	Tuesday	Wednesday	Thursday	Friday
8:00 A.M.–8:30 A.M.	Pick Me Up	Advisory	Pick Me Up	Advisory	Pick Me Up
8:30 A.M.–9:15 A.M.	Advisory	Travel to LTI	Advisory	Travel to LTI	Advisory
9:15 A.M.–12:00 P.M.	Advisory (cont'd)	LTI	Project work time	LTI	Advisory (cont'd)
12:00 P.M.–12:30 P.M.	Lunch	Lunch at LTI	Lunch	Lunch at LTI	Lunch
12:30 P.M.–1:30 P.M.	Academic Skills Workshop	LTI	Academic Skills Workshop	LTI	CSAP/ACT Prep
1:30 P.M.–2:15 P.M.	Project work time	Return to school	Advisory	Return to school	Project work time
2:15 P.M.–3:00 P.M.	Advisory	Advisory	Advisory	Advisory	Advisory

of this, each student will spend his or her time in a different way. Table 8.2 summarizes a typical Big Picture student learning experience.

The case study that follows shows how a Big Picture education all comes together.

Caleb: A Case Study

Caleb is a student in the senior class. He has been at our school since the ninth grade. Among his important personal characteristics, Caleb has been identified as twice-exceptional. He loves to read and write; when I first met him, he'd just finished Dante's *Inferno*, which he'd read for fun. He is also obsessed with Japanese military culture. Caleb's academic interest and personal passion is in the field of horticulture—he loves plants. He self-identifies math and procrastination as his biggest weaknesses. He loves music (mostly metal, but some hip-hop, too), and he is very into in-line "vert" skating, a pasttime that has caused more than one trip to the emergency room. By just about any standard, Caleb's a bright kid with a lot of potential—and just as many challenges.

Caleb's advisor, Jenna, has been with him since ninth grade as well. Their relationship has grown over the four years to a place where Caleb sees Jenna as both his teacher and his advocate. Jenna has more than once helped Caleb through difficult circumstances, including a brief period of homelessness and a struggle with foster care. She knows Caleb's family well, and throughout the four years she has tried to balance deep empathy with high expectations.

From the outset, Caleb seemed a perfect student for the Big Picture design. His passion for the plant world was already germinating in middle school, when he'd been involved in a community garden program and with a local nonprofit called The Urban Farm. His mother, Marie, had constantly battled the school system over Caleb's needs for intense support, both for his learning differences and his intellectual curiosity. In coming to our school, they found the right kind of environment for Caleb to explore his passions, receive help with his weaknesses, and explore his intellect.

In a college application written during his senior year, Caleb reflected on how he had been able to pursue his passions in high school:

> I spent all four years of my high school experience at a school that used the Big Picture learning model, a model which in the most abridged of explanations is one that promotes cultivation of personal character, learning through experience, and exploration of one's passions. As early as my freshman and sophomore years of high school I was already pursuing my passion for botanical research and horticulture on a professional level by writing propagation protocols, production schedules, and researching rare xeric species of plants for introduction at the botanic gardens. I pursued this passion throughout my secondary school experience and during my junior year acquired an internship at the university examining cuticular samples from New Guineaian flora in an effort to aid in the conservation of a tree kangaroo species that lives there. For the full duration of my four years of high school I have been presented with not only the challenges of high school but those of both the

professional and collegiate world as well; while I cannot say that I have come away from each challenge a success I can say that I met each challenge with the same intensity and utter resolve to succeed that I will meet the challenges of your university with.

Caleb's Learning Plan

The first component in creating Caleb's learning experience at our school is the Learning Plan. The main purpose it serves is as the placeholder document for the customized curriculum for the student. It outlines the learning targets, products, and practices the student is responsible for. It also is meant to align learning with content area standards. A portion of the Learning Plan includes methods of accountability, and is also used as the tool to hold the student accountable. Not seen as a static tool, it is a living, breathing document that can be revised and returned to over and over again. Finally, it is created by the Learning Plan Team, including student, advisor, family members, and mentor.

The Learning Plan in Table 8.3 is from Caleb's second trimester of eleventh grade. You'll notice that the first component on the Learning Plan is Caleb's internship: working with Dr. Chris Davidson at the university biology lab. That is the second element for our consideration.

Caleb's Internship

At a Big Picture school, the internship is where the proverbial rubber meets the road, because it is the one key component that must be based on the students' interests and passions. Over time, Caleb had narrowed his passions from the broad spectrum of "plants" to the narrower realm of "plant biology" to the specifics of "horticulture" to the minute "paleobotany." So his placement at a university biology research lab was the end result of significant learning and effort on his part.

Much of the burden for securing the internship is placed on the student. Students must explore their interests by doing research into career fields. They also have to conduct phone interviews, an activity that requires that they "cold call" a potential internship site to seek information. If the phone interview goes well, it may lead to an informational interview, usually a half-hour face-to-face meeting with a professional in the workplace. Informational interviews require a good deal of planning, and students have to practice in role-playing scenarios before they have their first one. A successful informational interview can lead to a Shadow Day, a chance for the student to spend about four hours alongside a professional at his or her job site. If the Shadow Day is a success, it leads to the Learning Through Internship (LTI). Obviously, it requires dedication and effort on the part of the student—both to get one and to keep one.

In Caleb's case, he met his mentor, Dr. Davidson, at a conference on botany research. It was a natural fit, given that Caleb had his interests narrowed so clearly.

One of the most important criteria in finding a good internship is the authenticity of the work and learning the student will be doing. There must be an authentic learning experience available for the student—not just work study. Too often high school internships are glorified work programs, where students trade time in the classroom for time filing, emptying the trash, stuffing envelopes, or answering the phone. A Big Picture Internship requires that the student be able to gain exposure to both the professional standards and expectations of the workplace and the complex academic learning expected at a college-prep high school. For Caleb, his internship placement in Dr. Davidson's research lab provides both a chance to work as a research scientist and the expectation to learn at a high level.

Finding a site that supports learning is of critical importance. It requires both a context for learning and a willing mentor. If both of these are in place, then the third element that must be available is a project through which the student gains knowledge and expertise. For Caleb, the work that Dr. Davidson was doing was right up his alley.

Take a look at the learning objectives identified by Caleb, Jenna, and Dr. Davidson in Table 8.4.

Notice that Caleb is going to be responsible for learning content (column 1), developing new skills (column 2), and engaging with a new community (column 3). It's the combination of these three sets of expectations that leads to the rigor we're after in our school.

Table 8.3. Caleb's Learning Plan

Learning Plan 11.2	Student: Caleb Robinson	LTI Site: Dept. of Biology		Advisor: Jenna Mackie		Mentor: Dr. Chris Davidson	
My Work	What will I show @ my exhibition?	Empirical Reasoning	Quantitative Reasoning	Communication	Social Reasoning	Personal Qualities	Progress/ Expectations
Title and description or attach Project Proposal	Evidence	What will you learn to do? OR To what questions will you learn the answers?					Completed or incomplete? Evaluation?
LTI Search, Work, Projects							
LTI Project: Determining the diet of tree kangaroos through fecal samples	Slides, Slide workshop	Improve my slide making skills (more efficient, 3 or 4 a week) (ER) Higher percentage of perfect cuticles on my slides (ER)					
Independent Projects							
Physics Project	Power point outlining history of physics, explanation of four forces, explanation of particles; Book; notes; questions with answers from resources	History of physics (SR) Mechanics of physics and how they interact in our world (ER) Forces and Particles (ER) Developing framing questions (CM) Using quality resources to find answers to framing questions (PQ) Reading and note taking (reading strategies) (CM)					

		Big Picture 301 Focus
Organization of work to do and work completed	Email account	Self-discipline (PQ)
Time management: remembering to tell people things ahead of time and knowing what is due ahead of time	Daily list, Day planner	Self-discipline (PQ)
		Advisory / Workshops
Math Workshop	Work and assessments	Probability (QR)
		College Class
College Class 1: ENG 121	Creative narrative, Summary response	Different types of essays (CM) Improving style, structure, and writing in general (CM)
College Class 2: Paleo-botany	Term paper, Exams, Book, Notes, Discussion on Dino, Paper	Development of plant life on earth from the Pre-Cambrian to the present (ER, SR) To take essay exams (CM) College level reading (CM)
College Class 3: Advanced Topics in Developmental Biology	Final Project, Book	How the genetic tool kit has evolved (SR, ER) How to explain animal diversity using the genetic tool kit (SR, ER)

Table 8.4. Caleb's Learning Objectives

Content	Skills and Habits (Learning Goal)	Character and Community Requirements
Anatomical structure in plant cuticles	Research paper writing (communication, empirical reasoning)	Responsibility and communication when in need of help
Biology of tree kangaroos	Reading nonfiction (communication)	Interactions with graduate and undergraduate students
Vegetation of New Guinea	Operation of microscope slides	
	Use of research microscope with digital camera	
	Using PowerPoint (communication)	
	Preparation of leaf material to provide slides for microscope (empirical reasoning)	
	Time management (personal qualities)	
	Organization (personal qualities)	

Another critical element of the Big Picture Internship is the presence of multiple layers of accountability. We're looking for a scenario that holds the student accountable to both academic and professional standards. In Caleb's case, he has to demonstrate that he understands the content (e.g., anatomy of plant cuticles, diet of tree kangaroos) to meet the professional standards established by Dr. Davidson. He also has to work with Jenna, his advisor, to complete his work and compile evidence to show that he has met the state standards. And because the work he is doing is in connection with a project that Dr. Davidson is completing, he also has to reach the higher standard of creating content that can be used for academic publication.

We also want to make sure that the internship site and the mentor benefit from hosting one of our students. Thus, we require that a component of what the Big Picture student does contributes value to the internship site. In Caleb's case, his work was integral to a study that Dr. Davidson hoped to complete and have published. Caleb became another assistant in that work.

Caleb's Project

The independent learning that takes place within a Big Picture school is only possible with a significant set of expectations put in place. We call these the 5 As.

- Authenticity—The project is real and provides benefit to the student and the audience.

- Active learning—The project requires a hands-on component and takes place outside of school.

- Adult relationships—In order to complete the project, the student needs to use adults to help, either as resources or as mentors.

- Academic rigor—The project is challenging and complex, requiring the student to learn new content, master prior knowledge, and expand into new areas of study.

- Assessment—The project is planned to include the standards by which it will be evaluated, a time line for completion, and the targeted product or outcome.

In Caleb's case, his project is to determine the diet of tree kangaroos by analyzing fecal samples. He completed a project proposal that outlines how he will carry out his work:

Project Proposal

Student: Caleb Robinson

Year/Tri: 11.1

Internship: Department of Biology

Advisor: Jenna Mackie

Parent: Ms. Walker

Mentor: Dr. Chris Davidson

Project Title/Topic: Determining the Diet of Tree Kangaroos from Fecal Samples

1. Main Product: A poster presentation perhaps with an oral presentation. This poster will be presented at the undergraduate research symposium.

2. Other Evidence

   a. Project proposal with time line 9/14

   b. Tree kangaroo research paper 10/4

c. Three slides to illustrate mastery of mounting 9/27

d. Fifteen slides of the species from New Guinea 11/10

e. Ninety-seven slides of species done second trimester

f. Group them by physical characteristics of the cuticle second trimester

g. Working with Lucid to build a "Key" third trimester

h. Research outline third trimester

i. Research write-up third trimester

j. Do poster in PowerPoint third trimester

k. Present at symposium 5/15

3. Learning Objectives (Table 8.5)

4. Framing Questions for Research

1. What are Matschie's tree kangaroos eating in the rainforest of New Guinea?

2. What modifications are necessary to the standard technique of cuticle preparation?

Table 8.5. Learning Objectives Aligned to Big Pictures Goals*

Content	Skills and Habits	Character and Community
Anatomical structure in cuticles	Research paper writing (CM, ER)	Responsibility and communication when he needs help
Biology of tree kangaroos	Reading non-fiction (CM)	Interactions with undergrad and graduate students
Vegetation of New Guinea Highlands	Operation of microscope slides	Teamwork
	Use of research microscope with digital camera	
	Using PowerPoint (CM)	
	Preparation of leaf material to provide materials for microscope (ER)	
	Time management (PQ)	
	Organization (PQ)	

*Communication (CM); Social Reasoning (SR); Empirical Reasoning (ER); Quantitative Reasoning (QR); Personal Qualities (PQ).

5. Resources

   Dr. Davidson

   Gordon Peters

   Tree Kangaroos

   The Anatomy of Dicots

   Reference collection at University Library

   Lucid

   PowerPoint

   Adobe Photo Shop

The 5 As

1. Authenticity: Conservation is authentic, and it is a research project Dr. Davidson undertook and needs help completing.

2. Active Learning: I will be able to answer questions by doing scientific experiments, using microscopes, and doing original research.

3. Academic Rigor: The cuticle keeps falling apart; tons of reading; college level reading, research, and writing; real-life application of time management; exposure to advanced optical equipment used in research labs.

4. Adult Relationships: I have to work with Gordon, a PhD student, and Dr. Davidson three times a week. We work very closely.

5. Assessment:

   a. Quality of slide set (real world standards)

   b. Poster (real world academic standard)

   c. Ability to discuss that poster

   d. I will present my work at my exhibitions where my advisor, mentors, peers, and family will be able to critique my work.

   e. I will write a reflective narrative each trimester to document my growth and learning.

   f. My advisor will write a narrative each trimester; she will document my growth and learning.

g. My mentors will fill out evaluation forms and provide feedback.

h. We hope to create a rubric for the final product.

In order to satisfy the objective of learning about tree kangaroo biology, Caleb wrote a paper for Dr. Davidson to demonstrate what he'd learned: Matschie's tree kangaroos are usually considered herbivores, although they have been known in some cases to eat insects and the eggs and young of birds. The main portion of their diet consists of leaves, but they will also feed upon flowers, fruits, nuts, bark, and sap. In the zoo they are fed fruit leaves, apples, carrots, corn, kale, timothy hay, spinach leaves, alfalfa, lettuce, celery, and hard-boiled eggs. Tree kangaroos are also fed tea leaves to make up for the tannin present in the leaves they eat in the wild. Without those tea leaves the color of their coats would fade.

Evaluating Caleb's Work

We frequently evaluate student work at a Big Picture school. There are three main vehicles for this: exhibition, advisor narrative evaluation, and student reflective evaluation.

Exhibition is the process by which a student presents a portfolio of evidence to a panel of evaluators. The panel is usually made up of the members of the Learning Plan Team, including the advisor, the mentor, and parents or other family members. Other students, community members, and other teachers can also be part of the panel.

The main point of the exhibition is to have the student answer the question, "What have you learned?" through showing evidence. Exhibitions are held at the end of each trimester, or more frequently if the student and Learning Plan Team think it would be beneficial. The presentation gives an overview of the progress the student has made with respect to the goals on the Learning Plan. Panelists are able to determine whether the student has met the goals on the LP, or if more work is needed. In this way, the exhibition is both a formative and a summative assessment, and is used as the catalyst for the next iteration of the Learning Plan to be developed for the next grading period.

Advisor narrative evaluation is the process by which the advisor provides written feedback to the student and his or her parents about the progress the student made during that trimester. Often the advisor must balance the need for praise with the need to provide critical feedback. An excerpt from what Jenna wrote about Caleb at the end of the second trimester of his junior year is helpful:

> Caleb feels that math is his weakness. He feels "dumb" in math. But every time I work with Caleb, I notice that he has an aptitude for mathematical problem solving. He may not arrive at the answer the prescribed way that the teachers teach, but he figures it out and usually understands it because he truly thinks about the problem and understands it. Caleb is NOT DUMB in math. I wish he could see that in fact he is quite good at it. Perhaps then he would work on it more and see improvement.

The advisor narrative evaluation serves as an excellent running record of a student's progress over the course of his or her education. It also creates a wonderful narrative arc when each individual document can be read as part of the cumulative story. In reading Jenna's appraisal of Caleb's math struggles, one gets the sense of just how familiarly she knows him. When conveyed to parents and students, this level of being known well really makes an impression.

The student also must reflect on his or her learning for the trimester. This student reflective narrative can sometimes serve as a place to crow about one's accomplishments, and just as often it is the forum for the *mea culpa* that the student needs to offer. Caleb wrote the following in response to the second trimester exhibition of his junior year:

> You always manage to find a way to snatch defeat from the jaws of victory" a good friend once told me over a game of chess. Aside from damning him to hell for making it, I'd never stopped to consider the biting but accurate observation of this maven sage. Now that I sit here writing my narrative, I realize that that is the perfect way to sum up my exhibition: I politely walked into the room and clubbed the victory I had so lovingly nurtured for 12 weeks over the head until it regurgitated defeat all over my shoes. . . . The cruel irony of this story is that I was in fact looking forward to my exhibition. There were

times when I would be up working until four in the morning and my only way of justifying my misery was by telling myself, "at least my exhibition will be good." Ultimately, I think the huge difference in what I wanted my exhibition to be and what it was is about 70% my fault. If I had a better understanding of logical progression and better presentation skills perhaps the time constraints wouldn't have been so profound. When it's all said and done I feel as though I did my job this trimester. All my work got done and I had the strongest trimester I've had yet. However, I think that having a practice run for my exhibition next trimester wouldn't be a bad idea.

There is a level of honesty in Caleb's evaluation that doesn't show up in most forms of assessment. He obviously has a sense of humor about it, but takes responsibility for poorly exhibiting what he considers to be some of his best work.

Caleb's Results

In many ways Caleb is a typical Big Picture student. He had struggled just as much as he had succeeded in school before coming to us. He had lofty goals and exceptional talent, but limited prospects for achieving them in a traditional, comprehensive high school. Only through the structures and processes in place at a Big Picture school was he able to thrive academically. By being in a small high school that placed equal value on personal advocacy and academic achievement, Caleb has had a high school education that has been rigorous *and* personalized. Here is how he put it in his college essay:

Perhaps the most important lesson that Jenna taught me is that anything worth doing is worth doing to the best of one's ability. Before I met Jenna I was a classic underachiever doing just enough to get by. To me the difference between an A and a C was purely a matter of semantics. One of the most heated arguments Jenna and I ever had was over an assignment she refused to accept because of an obvious lack of effort. I kindly pointed out that even with the "obvious lack of effort" my paper was still better than everyone else's, and if she hated it so badly she could just take off points. What did I care? I would pass regardless. It was at that point that Jenna had a long discussion with me about how "passing" was relative and that by merely meeting the standard, I was passing as a student but failing as a person. I redid the paper, and ever since that day, I have tried my hardest to pass as a student and a person not only in school but in life as well.

Caleb graduated in May 2007. His academic and personal achievements were worthy of admission to one of the most selective liberal arts colleges in the nation; he also earned a full scholarship for all four years.

Lessons Learned

What we do in a Big Picture school isn't necessarily unique. Many small schools have learning plans, assess learning through presentations assessment, use portfolios of student work, combine experiences with academics for learning, and organize around advisories. And students in many small schools are able to achieve extraordinary things. Yet it is the way we combine those essential components in the Big Picture design that creates the "perfect storm" of learning, learning that under the best of circumstances is both highly personalized and highly rigorous.

Reflection Questions

1. What would it take for your school to provide opportunities for students to dig deeply into subjects they find intriguing?

2. What kind of flexibility over time and exploration of traditional subject matter would you need in order to allow for personalized learning?

3. How would your school build rubrics and assessments to ensure that student learning is rigorous? Could the rubrics and assessments be aligned to meet state standards as demonstrated in Chapter Eight?

4. Could this kind of learning experience help keep more high-risk students engaged in school so they graduate on time?

Resources

Benitez, M., Davidson, J., Flaxman, L., Sizer, T., & Sizer, N. (2009). *Small Schools, Big Ideas: The Essential Guide to Successful School Transformation.* San Francisco: Jossey-Bass.

The Big Picture Company, www.bigpicture.org

DiMartino, J., & Clarke, J. (2008). *Personalizing the High School Experience for Each Student.* Alexandria, VA: ASCD.

DiMartino, J., Clarke, J., & Wolk, D. (eds.) (2003). *Personalized Learning: Preparing High School Students to Create Their Futures.* Lanham, MD: Rowman & Littlefield.

Grabelle, S., & Littky, D. (2004). *The Big Picture: Education Is Everyone's Business.* Alexandria, VA: ASCD.

Levine, E. (2001). *One Kid at a Time: Big Lessons from a Small School.* New York: Teachers College Press.

CONCLUSION

Joseph A. DiMartino and Denise L. Wolk

Throughout this book, we have examined the promising practices taking place in a handful of innovative schools throughout the country. Although a few are chronicled here, there are many more schools involved in making change every day by implementing the kinds of activities that these schools have used.

Each of the student contributors to our book emphasized the importance of personalization in their school success whether in a large city or a small town. Having at least one adult who knows them well over a prolonged period of time can make all the difference in a student's life. I mentioned before that my own son graduated from the Metropolitan Career and Technical Center (The Met) in Providence in 2008, and although he was the poster child for the reluctant, resistant learner, his advisor and project mentors made all the difference in keeping him engaged and on track for graduation. The irony is this isn't rocket science—it is often the use of simple common sense and a human touch that motivates students and helps them to determine their own way.

In the introduction we referenced *The Call to Action: Transforming High School for All Youth,* produced by The National High School Alliance, and six core principles for student success. All of the schools included in our book embody those core principles. By creating personalized learning environments students have opportunities to know their teachers and each other well. By working to provide opportunities for academic engagement for all, school staff find creative ways to spark the intellectual curiosity in students who are not naturally capable of advocating for themselves. Empowering educators to use innovative practices to challenge students to take intellectual risks and to create communities of learners among both students and staff is a hallmark of innovative and accountable leaders. The payoff comes when the wider community becomes engaged in the life of the school and students are offered additional opportunities outside the school walls. Finally by providing an integrated system of high standards, curriculum, instruction, assessments, and supports these schools provide students with a world-class education.

The Center for Secondary School Redesign (CSSR) has created a vision of what the twenty-first century American high school should become. We present this vision, which reflects the practices featured in this book, here. It incorporates the basic principles presented in the National High School Alliance's *Call to Action* but provides more detail about what a school can do to become a high performing twenty-first century school.

The Center for Secondary School Redesign (CSSR) List of Practices

The following practices are proven to lead to enhanced student outcomes regarding the achievement of twenty-first century skills, civic and social development, and postsecondary readiness and success.

A. Leadership and Governance

1. The school principal provides leadership in the school community by building and maintaining a vision, direction, and focus for student learning.

2. The principal creates and works with a site-based leadership team and employs sound change leadership processes.

3. The school is governed by a site council, which is all-inclusive, diverse, and comfortable so students, parents, and members of the staff are willing to participate. (In high schools students who are representative of the demographic and academic backgrounds of the student body comprise a majority of the site council.)

4. The high school community, which cannot be value-neutral, advocates and models a set of core values essential in a democratic

and civil society, including an appreciation for the diversity of the American populace.

5. In conjunction with agencies in the community, the school helps coordinate the delivery of physical and mental health and social services for youth.

6. Recognizing that education is a continuum, high schools reach out to elementary and middle level schools, as well as institutions of higher education, to better serve the articulation of student learning and to ensure that those at each stage of the continuum understand what will be required of students at the succeeding stage.

B. Professional Community

1. Members of the staff collaborate in both interdisciplinary and discipline-specific teams, including staff and (in high schools) students to develop and implement the school's learning goals.

2. Common planning time is regularly scheduled and amounts to 30 minutes for every hour of instruction.

3. The school is a professional learning community that focuses on the skills and knowledge required to ensure that the principal, teachers, and other staff members continuously improve in their ability to address students' intellectual and affective needs as they relate to improved student outcomes.

C. Personalized Learning

1. Students display a sense of belonging and the feeling that someone cares whether they are doing well in academic, civic, and social realms.

2. Each student has a Personal Plan for Progress reflective of the individual learning styles, histories, interests, and aspirations that documents an engaging process of student introspection, goal setting, community-based explorations, progress review, and reflection, all demonstrated through biannual student-led conferences.

3. Every high school student will have a Personal Adult Advocate that meets with him or her either individually or in a small group daily to help him or her personalize the educational experience. Advisory content includes preparing students for the college admissions process, including the completion of the FAFSA (Free Application for Federal Student Aid).

4. The students' families are engaged as partners in the students' education, especially as participants in student-led conferences and as reviewers of exhibitions.

D. Personalized Teaching

1. To promote a culture of high expectations for all, students are heterogeneously grouped in all subject areas.

2. Teachers teaching AP and honors classes are responsible for contact time with no more than 100 students per school year, and teachers teaching more challenging students are responsible for contact time with no more than 60 students per school year.

3. Role model teachers teach the most challenging students, e.g., freshmen.

4. The school employs a flexible schedule that allows better use of time in order to meet the individual needs of students to ensure academic success.

5. Teachers design high-quality work and teach in ways that engage students, cause them to persist, and, when the work is successfully completed, result in their satisfaction and their acquisition of knowledge, critical thinking and problem-solving skills, and other abilities valued by society.

6. Teachers are adept at acting as coaches and facilitators to promote more active involvement of students in their own learning.

7. Teachers know and use a variety of strategies and settings that identify and accommodate individual learning styles, increase literacy levels, and engage students.

E. Personalized Curriculum

1. The school eliminates the Carnegie unit in favor of exhibitions of mastery as the basis for earning credit.

2. The school identifies a set of essential learnings in which students must demonstrate achievement in order to graduate, to include student outcome expectations in academic, civic, and social realms.

3. The high school has only three departments, STEM (Science, Technology, Engineering, and Mathematics), Humanities, and Community Connected Learning in order to integrate the school's curriculum and emphasize depth over breadth of coverage.

4. The content of the curriculum connects to real-life applications of knowledge and skills, including internships, service learning, and project-based learning opportunities.

5. The school has partnerships with institutions of higher education that includes dual-enrollment opportunities for all students.

6. The core curriculum is college preparatory for all and is aligned with the admissions requirements with the flagship state university in the state.

7. Each course offers an honors challenge that is inquiry-based and available to any student who chooses to complete the work.

8. Students construct knowledge through projects designed to require students to access knowledge, analyze it, synthesize it, and present it as a body of material which he or she has designed to maximize communication with students, teachers, and community members.

9. The school has plans to make technology integral to curriculum, instruction, and assessment, accommodating different learning styles and helping teachers to individualize and improve the learning process.

F. Personalized Assessment

1. At the heart of the school is performance assessment that permits teachers to have deep knowledge of their students and the practices that would best help them to learn.

2. Comprehensive personal learning plans, graduation challenge, capstone, senior projects, portfolio assessments all including exhibitions are the norm and required of every student.

3. Assessment is incorporated into instruction so that assessment is accomplished using a variety of methods and does not merely measure students, but becomes part of the learning process.

4. Assessment practices capture the dynamic and varied ways in which a student's academic growth occurs—in other words, more closely resembles a videotape than a single snapshot.

As the National High School Alliance asserted in the *Call to Action*, in order for schools to effectively meet the needs of their students in these demanding times, the design of the school must be appropriate for the community in which it resides. All of the schools in this book have deeply addressed each of the major sections of the CSSR vision, but each has done so in ways that are quite unique to its communities.

Public schools across the nation are facing extreme economic conditions, and there is a great deal of pressure to allow the gains that have been made in personalized learning to be set aside to close budget gaps, or to close schools that aren't improving test scores quickly enough to satisfy the Adequate Yearly Progress (AYP) requirements in No Child Left Behind. The pressure is particularly strong in low-performing urban districts, and "fixing" failing schools has become a key focal point for educational policy. Charter schools are also favored, and they have already become the fastest growing option for implementing reform. In the 2009–2010 school year, there were already more than 5,000 charter schools nationwide, with 419 new charter schools opened in 39 states and the District of Columbia.

All of the schools in this book have implemented practices and reforms that have improved educational outcomes for hundreds of thousands of students across the country. Most of them are charter schools. We hope that school leaders, teachers, parents, students, and community members will take these lessons to heart as the next wave of change comes.

APPENDIX: SCHOOL AND ORGANIZATION CONTACT INFORMATION

Schools

Boston Arts Academy
174 Ipswich Street
Boston, MA 02215
(617) 635–6470
www.bostonartsacademy.org

**Federal Hocking
     High School**
8461 State Route 144
Stewart, OH 45778
(740) 662–3211
www.federalhocking.k12.oh.us

**Francis W. Parker Charter
     Essential School**
49 Antietam Street
Devens, MA 01434
(978) 772–3293
www.parker.org

**Front Range Early College
     High School**
601 E 64th Avenue
Denver, CO 80229
(303) 853–1960
www.mapleton.us

Granger High School
315 Mentzer Avenue
Granger, WA 98932
(509) 854–1705
www.gsd.wednet.edu

Madison High School
4833 Doliva Drive
San Diego, CA 92117
(858) 496–8410
www.sandi.net/schools/high/madison

Minnesota New Country School
210 Main Street
Henderson, MN 56044
(507) 248–3353
www.newcountryschool.com

New Technology High School
920 Yount Street
Napa, CA 94559
(707) 259–8557
www.newtechhigh.org

School of the Future
127 E. 22nd Street
New York, NY 10010
(212) 475–8086
www.sof.edu

Organizations

Center for Secondary School Redesign
621 Wakefield Street
West Warwick, RI 02893
(401) 828–0077
www.cssr.us

Educators for Social Responsibility
23 Garden Street
Cambridge, MA 02138
(800) 374–2645
www.esrnational.org

ABOUT THE EDITORS

Joseph A. DiMartino is founder and president of the Center for Secondary School Redesign, Inc. (CSSR). Under his leadership CSSR has become a leading provider of groundbreaking technical assistance to support both policy change and change leadership at the district and school level, thus leading to a richer secondary school experience for all youth. He coauthored, with John Clarke, the highly acclaimed book, *Personalizing the High School Experience for Each Student,* published by the Association for Supervision and Curriculum Development (ASCD) in 2008. He also consulted with ASCD in the creation of the video series *High Schools at Work: Creating Student-Centered Learning* and also cowrote an accompanying facilitators guide. Primarily because of his leadership in the development of *Breaking Ranks II* and his contributions to *Breaking Ranks in the Middle,* Joe was given the distinguished Service to Education Award by the National Association of Secondary School Principals (NASSP) in 2006. He was named a DiFelice Scholar by Salem State College in Salem, Massachusetts, in 2007.

Prior to the founding of CSSR, Joe served for nearly a decade as director of the Secondary School Redesign program of the Education Alliance at Brown University, where he was instrumental in maintaining the university's leadership role in the national conversation about redesigning high schools. At Brown, Joe oversaw the design, development, and implementation of numerous research and technical assistance projects promoting high school redesign. Much of his effort went into the development of the Breaking Ranks Process of comprehensive high school reform, which has been implemented in over 40 schools across the country.

From 2002 through 2005, Joe served as chair of the steering committee of the National High School Alliance. He served as co-chair of the National Task Force on the High School and the Breaking Ranks 2 Commission of NASSP. In this role, Joe directed the creation of *Breaking Ranks 2: Strategies for Leading High School Reform*. He also served on both the National Urban Task Force and the Breaking Ranks in the Middle Commission of NASSP, and is currently serving on the strategic advisory board of *the.News* at MacNeil/Lehrer Productions.

Joe's efforts to promote policy reforms that can lead to high school redesign include supporting Rhode Island's statewide high school reform efforts. This work includes the creation of a statewide vision of a twenty-first century high school and the development of an assessment system and the provision of technical supports to districts implementing the newly mandated graduation requirements. Joe also supported statewide high school reform efforts in Maine, Connecticut, Vermont, and New Hampshire. He provided leadership and research support to the New England Association of Schools and Colleges' Commission on Public Secondary Schools in the development of standards for high school accreditation of nearly 700 high schools throughout the region.

Joe is first and foremost a parent, often stating that he has learned much more from his children, including the four that were adopted from outside the United States, than he could ever hope to teach them. His children are a diverse bunch including two biological children, two Asians, and two Latin Americans. Three of the adoptees joined the DiMartino family when they were between six and twelve years of age. It is through the lens of their experiences that Joe became devoted to working with and advocating for the educational opportunities afforded to diverse adolescents in a variety of settings. Whether involving a playing field, classroom, or vocational placement, Joe has worked to ensure that individual youth have a voice in their education. He has utilized his role as parent, coach, mentor, and advocate to get to know hundreds of adolescents, and his passion for connecting with them continues.

Joe earned a bachelor's degree from Brown University and a Master's in Education from Rhode Island College; he has completed all the coursework for a Doctor of Philosophy in Culturally Responsive Education from Brown University. He is an adjunct faculty member at Rhode Island College, where he has taught courses in High School Personalization.

Denise L. Wolk is a senior program associate and director of publications and communications at Educators for Social Responsibility, an organization dedicated to helping educators create safe, caring, respectful, and productive learning environments. Her duties include providing coaching and training on high school redesign elements, including advisory design and implementation, as well as production for various ESR publications. Prior to joining ESR, Denise served as a program associate in the Secondary School Redesign program at The Education Alliance at Brown University. Her work included researching and developing workshops directly tied to personalizing the experience for students in high schools. As a member of the SSR team at Brown, she served on the core work group with NASSP to write *Breaking Ranks II: Strategies for Leading High School Reform*, published in 2004, and also served as a member of the core group to write *Breaking Ranks in the Middle*, another NASSP project. Denise was also a contributor to the development of the workshop and publication *Changing Systems to Personalize Learning: Discover the Power of Advisories* (LAB, 2003), and has facilitated workshops and institutes with schools around the country.

Before joining the team at Brown, Denise served as a researcher/writer for the landmark "mapping project" to inform the National Alliance on the American High School by researching the various reforms occurring in high schools and the youth development efforts across the country. She was managing editor and a contributing author for the book *"Personalized Learning: Preparing High School Students to Create Their Futures"* (ScarecrowEducation, 2003) and provided extensive fact checking and editorial services for Dr. David Kessler's book *A Question of Intent* (Public Affairs Press, 2002). She spent more than 20 years in communications and management before refocusing her efforts on education reform.

A lifelong student, Denise studied journalism at Fresno City College and earned a Bachelor's Degree in Marketing from the University of Phoenix, and is still working on an MBA with a focus on education and nonprofit management. She lives with her family in Rhode Island.

Chapter One

Ricardo Leblanc-Esparza is the son of an immigrant agricultural worker and grew up in a town quite similar to Granger, only 20 miles away. At his father's urging, he threw himself into high school, both academically and athletically, winning a wrestling scholarship to Central Washington University, where he prepared to be a teacher and wrestling coach. He returned to the area with the mission of making sure students at Granger have the same opportunities he had. Ricardo and Granger High School have received numerous awards and recognition at the state and national levels. He has been a featured speaker for Education Trust, Model Schools National Conferences, and Academic Distinction Fund. He recently retired after nine years as principal of Granger High School and 25 years as an educator, and is working as a school change coach with the Center for Secondary School Redesign.

Chapter Two

Debbie Osofsky is the advisory coordinator of the Francis W. Parker Charter Essential School in Devens, Massachusetts, and through Parker's Theodore R. Sizer Teachers Center consults with other schools in various stages of implementing advisory programs. She is a former middle and high school teacher and has worked extensively with advisory programs at the schools in which she has taught. Debbie is the principal author of *Changing Systems to Personalize Learning: Discover the Power of Advisories,* a three day institute and publication of The Education Alliance at Brown University. Debbie has a Master's of Education in Risk and Prevention focusing on adolescence from Harvard University and a B.A. in History from Brown University.

Teri Schrader is principal of the Francis W. Parker Charter Essential School and Theodore R. Sizer Teachers Center, and is in her eleventh year at the school, where she began as lead teacher for Arts and Humanities. Prior to her arrival at Parker School, Teri taught for 14 years at the Watkinson School in Hartford, Connecticut, where she directed the Creative Arts Program and facilitated school-wide efforts to integrate and infuse the arts in all subject areas. A member of the National School Reform Faculty, she is a Critical Friends Group coach at Parker and a national facilitator for the work of developing Critical Friends Groups within schools aiming to make a difference in student achievement by developing the conditions for thoughtful and sustained professional growth of teachers. Teri is the author of "Who We Are and How It Translates to What We Do," published by Boston University's *Journal of Education* (vol. 185, Number 2, 2004), and a contributor to the book, *Sent to the Principal*, by Kathleen Cushman.

Chapter Three

Paul Curtis is responsible for defining and refining the New Tech High School model, which is increasingly being recognized in the United States as a national leader in producing twenty-first century students. Since 2002, the New Technology Foundation has been assisting in transferring the knowledge and experiences of the original school in Napa, California, to a growing network of New Tech schools in other communities seeking to replicate its results. Through this work, the Foundation has supported 35 communities in a variety of regions with an array of demographics who have chosen this model as the framework for their own school reinvention efforts. In 1997 Paul was recruited to New Technology High School and immediately saw the benefits of working in an environment that allows for block scheduling, team teaching, and, of course, a technology-rich classroom. While at New Tech High, he helped define the school's curriculum model, assessment practices, and technology tools that have become the hallmark of all New Technology High Schools. As the school gained a reputation for innovation and hosted hundreds of visitors each year, he became a strong advocate for school restructuring and educational reform. In 2000, Paul was selected as Napa County Teacher of the Year.

Chapter Four

Ron Newell is learning program and assessment director for the EdVisions Schools based in Henderson, Minnesota. Ron and partner Doug Thomas started EdVisions as a way to generate excitement in the teaching profession and to revitalize public education. They believed that if teachers were "owners" rather than simply employees, they would have more control and accountability, thus leading to higher-performing teachers, students, and educational institutions. By 2003, EdVisions Cooperative (the Coop) included a network of 10 charter schools, 125 teachers, and a few other members. The Coop currently provides teachers with payroll and benefits and plans to expand its role to areas such as charter school development and planning, as well as faculty and staff professional development. In 2000, Thomas and Newell started EdVisions, Inc. (the Inc.), an arm of the Coop, which sought to replicate the EdVisions learning model both regionally and nationally with grants from The Bill & Melinda Gates Foundation.

Mark Van Ryzin is a Ph.D. student in Educational Psychology at the University of Minnesota-Twin Cities. His research interests include innovation in education, adolescent development, teacher-student relationships, and teacher education and professional development. Mark received his M.A. in Educational Psychology from the University of Minnesota in 2006, and his master's thesis addressed motivation and psychological development in secondary school. Mark's work has been published in the *Journal of Comparative Psychology* and the *Journal of School Psychology,* and he has presented at a number of conferences, including the annual meeting of the American Educational Research Association (AREA), the biennial meeting of the Society for Research in Child Development (SRCD), and the Gates Foundation's Emerging Research Symposium. In addition to his schoolwork, Mark serves as a consultant to Education-Evolving and EdVisions, and is a member of the Advisory Board for Growth & Justice and the Minnesota Alliance with Youth.

Chapter Five

Catherine DeLaura was assistant principal and principal of School of the Future from 2002 to 2007. SOF is a Coalition of Essential Schools Mentor School located in New York City. She taught ESL and history as a Peace Corps volunteer and in the New York City public schools for 10 years. Her administration experience also includes founding an interdisciplinary arts program at Taft High School in the South Bronx and receiving an MBA from Columbia Business School. Her fundamental belief in the importance of school leadership for improving instruction and student achievement has led her to present workshops on curriculum planning, differentiation, and alternative assessment at various national conferences and to co-teach an Educational Leadership course to Aspiring Principals at Baruch College, CUNY. She is an NSRF endorsed facilitator and she is the mentor principal for a new CES secondary school in New York City.

Chapter Six

Virginia (Ginger) Eves' involvement in education not only spans more than three decades, it also includes hands-on experience in all grade levels, elementary through university. Ginger has served as a teacher, counselor, guidance supervisor, secondary assistant principal, high school principal, and district administrator. While serving as principal at Madison High, Ginger implemented small learning communities—one of which became an award-winning pre-engineering academy, Design and Technology, and a second one, School of the Arts, which resulted in an $850,000 district-funded state-of-the-art renovation of the Performing Arts Center at that site. Her last assignment was director of College, Career, and Technical Education, as well as project manager for six alternative education programs for the San Diego Unified School District. In addition, she also acted as liaison to the secondary counseling programs and to four comprehensive high schools redesigned into eighteen small high schools.

Chapter Seven

Linda Nathan is the founding headmaster of the Boston Arts Academy, the city's first and only public high school for the visual and performing arts. Under her leadership, the school has won state, national, and international recognition and awards including a Massachusetts Compass Award, a "Breaking Ranks" award from the National Association of Secondary School Principals, and a Mentor School award from the Coalition of Essential Schools. BAA sends well over 90 percent of its graduates to college—all residents of the city of Boston. Linda was instrumental in starting Boston's first performing-arts middle school, and was a driving force behind the creation of Fenway High School, recognized nationally for its innovative educational strategies and school-to-work programs. She is also a co-founder and board member of the Center for Collaborative Education in Boston, a nonprofit education reform organization dedicated to creating more equitable and democratic schools. Linda holds a Doctorate in Education from Harvard University, a Master's in Education Administration from Antioch University, and a Master of Performing Arts from Emerson College.

Chapter Eight

Jeff Park is a school administrator and educational entrepreneur in Denver, Colorado. Since 2002, Jeff has founded three Big Picture Schools in the Denver metro area—Skyland Community High School, Mapleton Preparatory High School, and Front Range Early College. He has worked in educational reform since 1994 as a teacher, coach, researcher, trainer, curriculum developer, consultant, and principal. His experience includes work as a high school humanities teacher, and he has worked with populations ranging from highly gifted students to students in at-risk communities. He has been published on a variety of topics including brain-based research, teacher professional development, and engaging students in school change. Jeff's work was profiled by *Education Week* in the September 22, 2004, issue. He holds an M.A. in Education from the University of Denver.

INDEX